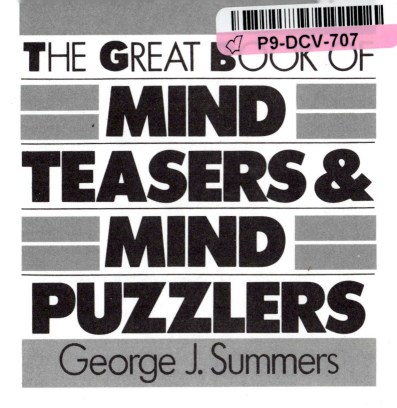

THE GREAT BOOK OF
MIND
TEASERS &
MIND
PUZZLERS

George J. Summers

Sterling Publishing Co., Inc.   New York

Library of Congress Cataloging-in-Publication Data

Summers, George J.
   The great book of mind teasers and mind puzzlers.

   "Combined edition of 'Mind Teasers' . . . and Mind
Puzzlers' ":—Verso CIP t.p.
   Includes index.
   1. Puzzles. 2. Detective and mystery stories.
I. Summers, George J. Mind teasers. 1986. II. Summers,
George J. Mind puzzlers. 1986. III. Title.
GV1507.D4S857 1986   793.73   85-27770
ISBN 0-8069-6320-4 (pbk.)

The Great Book of "Mind Teasers and Mind Puzzlers,"
copyright © 1986 by George J. Summers,
is a combined edition of "Mind Teasers" © 1977 and
"Mind Puzzlers" © 1984 by George J. Summers
Published by Sterling Publishing Co., Inc.
387 Park Avenue South, New York, N.Y. 10016
Distributed in Canada by Sterling Publishing
% Canadian Manda Group, P.O. Box 920, Station U
Toronto, Ontario, Canada M8Z 5P9
Distributed in Great Britain and Europe by Cassell PLC
Artillery House, Artillery Row, London SW1P 1RT, England
Distributed in Australia by Capricorn Ltd.
P.O. Box 665, Lane Cove, NSW 2066
Manufactured in the United States of America
All rights reserved

PART I
MIND TEASERS

Contents—Part I

Before You Begin Part I

The puzzles in **Part I** have been composed to resemble short whodunits. Each puzzle contains some "clues" and it is up to the reader, as "detective," to determine from these "clues" which of the various "suspects" is the "culprit."

The general method for solving these puzzles is as follows:

The question presented at the end of each puzzle contains a condition that must be satisfied by the solution. For example, "Who does not stand guard with Ida?" contains the condition "does not stand guard with Ida."

The "clues," numbered when there are more than one, also contain conditions; these conditions concern the various "suspects." The "detective" must use all of the conditions to determine the unique "culprit" that satisfies the condition contained in the question.

Read each of the puzzles through carefully and try to find the best way to approach it. If you don't know where to start, turn the page and read the hints provided to set you on the right track. These hints are (a) a Solution Scheme, for the reader who needs help in relating the puzzle to its solution, and (b) an Orientation, where it is needed, for the reader who needs help in interpreting the "clues." In addition, each of the first two puzzles is accompanied by a Discussion on how to solve it.

Possibly the most useful section for learning to solve logic puzzles successfully is found in the Solutions section in the back of **Part I**. As you complete a puzzle (or fail to answer it) and read the solution, follow the logical steps which were used to reach the conclusion provided. If you can follow the reasoning which eliminates the impossible choices until only the correct solution remains, then you will acquire the mastery needed to tackle any problem of logical deduction.

The Fight

Two of Anthony, Bernard, and Charles are fighting each other.

[1] The shorter of Anthony and Bernard is the older of the two fighters.

[2] The younger of Bernard and Charles is the shorter of the two fighters.

[3] The taller of Anthony and Charles is the younger of the two fighters.

Who is not fighting?

Solution Scheme and Discussion, page 8; Solution, page 92.

The Fight

SOLUTION SCHEME

SOLUTION SCHEME

Make a chart for yourself as follows:

Older fighter	Younger fighter	Taller fighter	Shorter fighter

Write "Anthony," "Bernard," or "Charles" in each box so that no condition is contradicted.

DISCUSSION

One could begin to solve this puzzle by making a table with headings as shown in the Solution Scheme and then by writing "A" (for Anthony), "B" (for Bernard), and "C" (for Charles) in as many ways as possible in the table like this:

Case	Older fighter	Younger fighter	Taller fighter	Shorter fighter
I	A	B	B	A
II	A	B	A	B
III	A	C	C	A
IV	A	C	A	C
V	B	A	A	B
VI	B	A	B	A
VII	B	C	C	B
VIII	B	C	B	C
IX	C	A	A	C
X	C	A	C	A
XI	C	B	B	C
XII	C	B	C	B

The next step would be to try to eliminate some cases using each of [1], [2], and [3] in turn: [1] explicitly eliminates cases II and VI, [2] explicitly eliminates cases VII and XI, and [3] explicitly eliminates cases IV and X. Now what? The person who is not fighting can still be either Anthony, Bernard, or Charles.

To get closer to the solution one must discover some *implied* conditions. From [1] it can be implied that Charles is not the older fighter, from [2] it can be implied that Anthony is not the shorter fighter, and from [3] it can be implied that Bernard is not the younger fighter. So [1] eliminates cases IX, X, XI, and XII; [2] eliminates cases I, III, VI, and X; and [3] eliminates cases I, II, XI, and XII.

So, from the earlier explicit conditions and the later implied conditions, the only remaining cases are V and VIII. Now what? The person who is not fighting can still be either Charles or Anthony.

To finally get to the solution, the relative heights of pairs of men can be compared from each of [1], [2], and [3] in turn for each of cases V and VIII. In one of these cases an impossible situation arises, namely, one man is both taller and shorter than another; so the case can be eliminated. From the one case remaining, the person who is not fighting can be determined.

The method just described is a tedious way to go about solving the puzzle because all the cases, twelve in number, are listed. Try to eliminate as many cases as possible before listing those remaining cases which involve more extended reasoning, but be careful that the list contains all those cases not yet eliminated.

See solution on page 92.

My Secret Word

One of the words listed below is my secret word.

AIM   DUE   MOD   OAT   TIE

With this list in front of you, if I were to tell you any one letter of my secret word, then you would be able to tell me the number of vowels in my secret word.

Which word is my secret word?

Orientation, Solution Scheme and Discussion, page 12; Solution, page 93.

The Tennis Players

Zita, her brother, her daughter, and her son are tennis players. As a game of doubles is about to begin:

[1] Zita's brother is directly across the net from her daughter.
[2] Her son is diagonally across the net from the worst player's sibling.

[3] The best player and the worst player are on the same side of the net.

Who is the best player?

Orientation and Solution Scheme, page 13;
Solution, page 93.

My Secret Word

"Any" in the second sentence enables you to determine my secret word.

SOLUTION SCHEME

Make a chart for yourself as follows:

A	D	E	I	M	O	T	U

Write "no" under each of the letters which cannot be in my secret word according to the condition given in the second sentence.

DISCUSSION

There are 256 possible ways that "no" could be written in the table. It is wise, then, to eliminate as many cases as possible, using the one "clue," before listing those remaining cases which involve more extended reasoning. Indeed, it turns out that only one case need be listed.

The Orientation tells the reader how to use the "clue." In other words, the "clue" says that *each* letter of my secret word is contained only in words having the same number of vowels. So M, for example, cannot be in my secret word because it is in AIM which has two vowels and in MOD which has only one vowel.

See solution on page 93.

The Tennis Players

ORIENTATION

Certain arrangements of four players on a tennis court are identical, though they appear to be different at first glance.

For example, 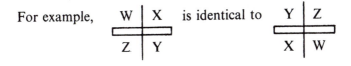 is identical to

because a rotation of one arrangement results in the other.

SOLUTION SCHEME

Make a diagram for yourself as follows:

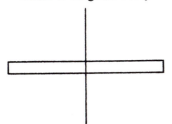

Write "Zita," "brother," "daughter," or "son" in each part of the tennis-court diagram so that no condition is contradicted.

After-Dinner Drink

Abigail, Bridget, and Claudia often eat dinner out.

[1] Each orders either coffee or tea after dinner.

[2] If Abigail orders coffee, then Bridget orders the drink that Claudia orders.

[3] If Bridget orders coffee, then Abigail orders the drink that Claudia doesn't order.

[4] If Claudia orders tea, then Abigail orders the drink that Bridget orders.

Who do you know always orders the same drink after dinner?

Orientation and Solution Scheme, page 16; Solution, page 94.

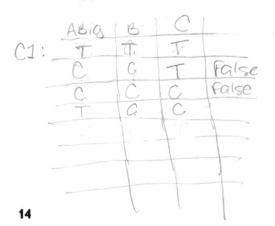

Abigail = tea

C1:

ABIG	B	C	
T	T	T	
C	C	T	False
C	C	C	False
T	C	C	

Equal Sums

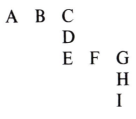

Each of the digits 1, 2, 3, 4, 5, 6, 7, 8, and 9 is:

[1] Represented by a different letter in the figure above.

[2] Positioned in the figure above so that each of A+B+C, C+D+E, E+F+G, and G+H+I is equal to 13.

Which digit does E represent?

*Orientation and Solution
Scheme, page 17;
Solution, page 95.*

After-Dinner Drink

ORIENTATION

From "If X orders milk, then Y orders milk" and "X orders milk," the only possible conclusion is "Y orders milk." From "If X orders milk, then Y orders milk" and "Y orders milk," more than one conclusion is possible: either "X orders milk" or "X does not order milk."

SOLUTION SCHEME

Make a chart for yourself as follows:

Abigail orders	Bridget orders	Claudia orders

Write "coffee" or "tea" in each box in as many ways as possible—crossing off any unused boxes—so that no condition is contradicted.

Equal Sums

ORIENTATION

A, B, C, and D are respectively and simultaneously interchangeable with I, H, G, and F; only E can be determined with certainty. Each of A, B, D, F, H, and I occurs in only one sum; each of C, E, and G occurs in two sums.

SOLUTION SCHEME

Make a diagram for yourself as follows:

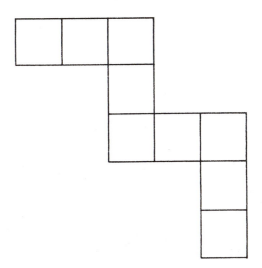

Write a digit in each box so that no condition is contradicted.

Relations

Lee, Dale, and Terry are related to each other.

[1] Among the three are Lee's legal spouse, Dale's sibling, and Terry's sister-in-law.

[2] Lee's legal spouse and Dale's sibling are of the same sex.

Who do you know is a married man?

*Orientation and Solution
Scheme, page 20;
Solution, page 95.*

X and O

The game of Tic-tac-toe is played in a large square divided into nine small squares.

[1] Each of two players in turn places his or her mark—usually X or O—in a small square.

[2] The player who first gets three marks in a horizontal, vertical, or diagonal line wins.

[3] A player will always place his or her mark in a line that already contains (a) two of his or her own marks or (b) two of his or her opponent's marks—giving (a) priority over (b).

Only the last mark to be placed in the game shown above is not given.

Which mark—X or O—wins the game?

Orientation and Solution Scheme, page 21;
Solution, page 96.

Relations

ORIENTATION

A person's sister-in-law may be the sister of that person's spouse or the wife of that person's brother.

SOLUTION SCHEME

Make a chart for yourself as follows:

Lee's spouse Sex M F	Dale's sibling Sex M F	Terry's sister-in-law Sex M F

Write "Lee," "Dale," or "Terry" in each box and indicate the sex of each person so that no condition is contradicted.

X and O

To determine which mark is the seventh mark to be placed in the game, you must determine which mark was the sixth mark placed in the game.

SOLUTION SCHEME

For convenience in discussing the puzzle, the squares can be numbered as follows:

1	2	3
4	5	6
7	8	9

Make a chart for yourself as follows:

The sixth mark placed in the game was in square number:	The seventh mark placed in the game was in square number:

Write the number of a square in each box so that no condition is contradicted.

Hint: "1" in the first box contradicts [3] because the X as a sixth mark would have been placed in square 5.

21

Names ☺

Miss Alden, Miss Brent, Miss Clark, Miss Doyle, and Miss Evans have short first and middle names.

[1] Four of them have a first or middle name of Fay, three of them have a first or middle name of Gay, two of them have a first or middle name of Kay, and one of them has a first or middle name of May.

[2] Either Miss Alden and Miss Brent are both named Kay or Miss Clark and Miss Doyle are both named Kay.

[3] Of Miss Brent and Miss Clark, either both are named Gay or neither is named Gay.

[4] Miss Doyle and Miss Evans are not both named Fay.

Who is named May?

Solution Scheme, page 24 ;
Solution, page 97.

Hockey Scores

The Angoras, the Bobcats, and the Cougars are hockey teams. In three games the Angoras played against the Bobcats, the Bobcats played against the Cougars, and the Angoras played against the Cougars.

[1] The three final scores of the games consisted of the numbers 1, 2, 3, 4, 5, and 6.

[2] The difference between the Angoras' higher score and the Bobcats' higher score was one more than the difference between the Bobcats' lower score and the Cougars' lower score.

[3] The highest total of a team's two scores was achieved by the team that lost the greatest number of games.

Which team achieved the highest total of its two scores?

Solution Scheme, page 25;
Solution, page 98.

Names

Make a chart for yourself as follows:

Alden	Brent	Clark	Doyle	Evans

Write "Fay," "Gay," "Kay," or "May" in each box so that no condition is contradicted.

Hockey Scores

SOLUTION SCHEME

Make a chart for yourself as follows:

Angoras versus Bobcats	

Angoras versus Cougars	

Bobcats versus Cougars	

Write "1," "2," "3," "4," "5," or "6" in each box so that no condition is contradicted.

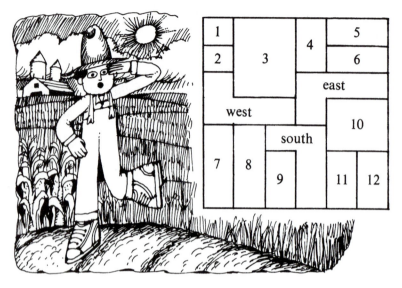

The Journey

The plan above shows an arrangement of corn, wheat, and rye fields. Jack is in the middle of one of the fields and has to meet his father in the middle of another field. On his journey from the field he is in to the field his father is in:

[1] His route takes him continuously through each of five other fields exactly once.

[2] He (being allergic to rye) avoids going through any part of a rye field.

[3] He notices no two fields of the same kind border on each other.

Which L-shaped field—east, west, or south—is a rye field?

*Orientation and Solution
Scheme, page 28;
Solution, page 98.*

The Visits

Alma, Bess, Cleo, and Dina visited Edna on Saturday.

[1] The time of each visit was as follows:

Alma at 8 o'clock,
Bess at 9 o'clock,
Cleo at 10 o'clock, and
Dina at 11 o'clock.

[2] At least one woman visited Edna between Alma and Bess.

[3] Alma did not visit Edna before both Cleo and Dina.

[4] Cleo did not visit Edna between Bess and Dina.

Who visited Edna last?

*Orientation and Solution
Scheme, page 29;
Solution, page 99.*

The Journey

ORIENTATION

The total number of fields involved in Jack's journey is seven.

SOLUTION SCHEME

Make a diagram for yourself as follows:

Assign each field to one of three arbitrary groups by marking like fields with one of three symbols. Find a route involving seven fields and marked with only two kinds of symbols.

The Visits

ORIENTATION

Each time mentioned may be either A.M. or P.M.

SOLUTION SCHEME

Make a chart for yourself as follows:

Order of visits				
Visiting times				

Write "Alma," "Bess," "Cleo," and "Dina" in some order along the top of the chart and the corresponding visiting times—"8," "9," "10," and "11"—below so that no condition is contradicted.

A Different Age

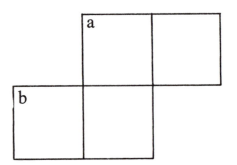

The ages of Ambrose, Brandon, and Chester can be related to the diagram above so that when just one digit is written in each box:

[1] a across is Ambrose's age in years.

[2] a down is the sum of Ambrose's age and Brandon's age in years.

[3] b across is the sum of Ambrose's age, Brandon's age, and Chester's age in years.

[4] Two of Ambrose, Brandon, and Chester are the same age in years.

Who is a different age in years from the other two?

Orientation and Solution Scheme, page 32; Solution, page 100.

The Doctor and the Lawyer

yeah :]

One of Mr. Horton, his wife, their son, and Mr. Horton's mother is a doctor and another is a lawyer.

[1] If the doctor is younger than the lawyer, then the doctor and the lawyer are not blood relatives.

[2] If the doctor is a woman, then the doctor and the lawyer are blood relatives.

[3] If the lawyer is a man, then the doctor is a man.

Whose occupation do you know?

Orientation and Solution Scheme, page 33; Solution, page 101.

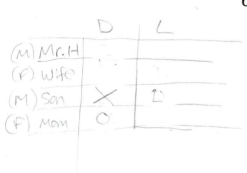

Mr. H = Doc
Wife : Lawyer

Mr. H = Doc
Son = Lawyer

Mr. H = Doc

A Different Age

ORIENTATION

The diagram is read like a standard crossword puzzle; assume no age can have a first digit of zero. There are many ways to complete the diagram.

SOLUTION SCHEME

Make a diagram for yourself as follows:

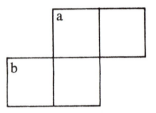

Write one digit in each box so that no condition is contradicted.

The Doctor and the Lawyer

ORIENTATION

In each numbered true statement:

Any assumption (an *if* part of a statement) that makes a conclusion (a *then* part of a statement) false must be a false assumption; any assumption that does not make a conclusion false may be true or false. "Doctor" and "lawyer" are placeholders for two unknown people; when a conclusion becomes false after substituting an ordered pair of people for "doctor" and "lawyer," the ordered pair must be the wrong pair.

SOLUTION SCHEME

Make a chart for yourself as follows:

Doctor	Lawyer

Write "Mr. Horton," "wife," "son," or "mother" in each box in as many ways as possible—crossing off any unused boxes—so that no condition is contradicted.

The Two Cubes

Here is a picture of two cubes:

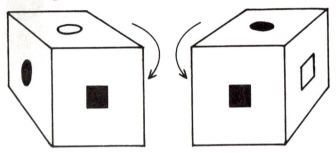

[1] The two cubes are exactly alike.

[2] The hidden faces indicated by the arrows have the same figure on them.

Which figure—○, ●, □, or ■ —is on the faces indicated by the arrows?

Orientation and Solution
Scheme, page 36;
Solution, page 101.

The Guards

Art, Bob, Cab, and Ida are guards in a museum.

[1] Each of Art, Bob, and Cab stands guard on exactly four days every week.

[2] Exactly two persons stand guard together every day.

[3] No person stands guard three days in a row.

[4] Here is a partial listing that shows when they stand guard every week:

Sun	Mon	Tues	Wed	Thurs	Fri	Sat
Art	Cab	Ida	Art	Bob	Cab	Ida
Bob	?	?	?	?	?	?
	B	C	B	I	A	C

Who does not stand guard with Ida?

Orientation and Solution
Scheme, page 37;
Solution, page 102.

The Two Cubes

ORIENTATION

The two identical cubes may be thought of as one cube in two different positions.

SOLUTION SCHEME

Draw a multiview cube as shown below.

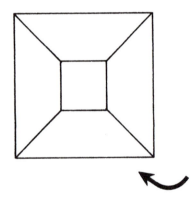

Place ○, ●, □, or ■
on each face of this multiview
cube and at the arrow (to
indicate the only face not seen)
so that no condition is contradicted.

The Guards

ORIENTATION

"Three days in a row" applies to any sequence of three days including (a) Friday, Saturday, and Sunday and (b) Saturday, Sunday, and Monday.

SOLUTION SCHEME

Make a chart for yourself as follows:

	Sun	*Mon*	*Tues*	*Wed*	*Thurs*	*Fri*	*Sat*
On guard	Art	Cab	Ida	Art	Bob	Cab	Ida
	Bob	?	?	?	?	?	?

Write "Art," "Bob," or "Cab" in each column so that no condition is contradicted.

Brothers

Amos, Bert, and Clem are brothers.

[1] Amos has exactly two brothers with grey eyes.

[2] Bert has exactly two brothers with grey or hazel eyes.

[3] Clem has exactly two brothers who do not have blue eyes.

[4] At least one of the three has hazel eyes and at least one of the three has blue eyes.

Whose eyes do you know the color of?

Orientation and Solution Scheme, page 40; Solution, page 103.

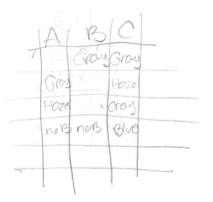

Equal Products

```
A       D
B   G   E
C       F
```

Each of seven digits from 0, 1, 2, 3, 4, 5, 6, 7, 8, and 9 is:

[1] Represented by a different letter in the figure above.

[2] Positioned in the figure above so that $A \times B \times C$, $B \times G \times E$, and $D \times E \times F$ are equal.

Which digit does G represent?

Orientation and Solution Scheme, page 41; Solution, page 104.

Brothers

ORIENTATION

The total number of brothers is not given.

SOLUTION SCHEME

Make a chart for yourself as follows:

Eye color of

Amos	Bert	Clem

Write "grey," "hazel," or "blue" in each box in as many ways as possible—crossing off any unused boxes—so that no condition is contradicted.

Equal Products

ORIENTATION

A and C are interchangeable, D and F are interchangeable, and each vertical row is interchangeable with the other—but not with the horizontal row; only G can be determined with certainty. Each of A, C, D, F, and G occurs in only one product; each of B and E occurs in two products.

SOLUTION SCHEME

Make a chart for yourself as follows:

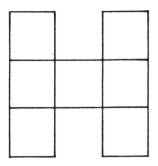

Write a digit in each box so that no condition is contradicted.

The Joker

A total of 21 cards consisting of 4 kings, 4 queens, 4 jacks, 4 tens, 4 nines, and 1 joker were dealt to Alec, Bill, and Carl. Then all jacks, tens, and nines were discarded. At that point:

[1] The combined hands consisted of 4 kings, 4 queens, and 1 joker.
[2] Alec had 2 cards, Bill had 3 cards, and Carl had 4 cards.
[3] The man with the most singletons did not have the joker.
[4] No man had more than 2 kings.

Who had the joker?

4K 4Q 1 jk [9]

Orientation and Solution Scheme, page 44; Solution, page 105.

The Joker

ORIENTATION
A hand contains a singleton when it contains only one king or only one queen or the joker.

SOLUTION SCHEME
Make a chart for yourself as follows:

Alec's hand	Bill's hand	Carl's hand

Cards:
4 kings
4 queens
1 joker

Identify the cards in each person's hand so that no condition is contradicted.

Tees and Els

Of Annette, Bernice, and Cynthia:

[1] Each belongs either to the Tee family whose members always tell the truth or to the El family whose members always lie.

[2] Annette says "Either I belong or Bernice belongs to a different family from the other two."

Whose family do you know the name of?

Solution Scheme, page 46;
Solution, page 104.

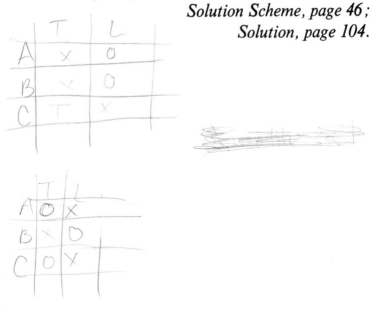

Tees and Els

SOLUTION SCHEME

Make a chart for yourself as follows:

If Annette's statement is	Then Annette belongs to the	And then Bernice and Cynthia, respectively, may belong to the
true	T	
false	F	

Write "Tee family" or "El family" in each box in the first column and "Tee family" or "El family" in as many ordered pairs as possible in each box in the second column so that no condition is contradicted.

Outre Ornaments

Outre Ornaments, Inc. sells baubles, gewgaws, and trinkets; while there I spoke to three different salespeople.

[1] The first salesperson I talked to told me any 7 baubles together with any 5 gewgaws have the same value as any 6 trinkets.

[2] The second salesperson I talked to told me any 4 baubles together with any 9 trinkets have the same value as any 5 gewgaws.

[3] The third salesperson I talked to told me any 6 trinkets together with any 3 gewgaws have the same value as any 4 baubles.

[4] When I bought some of each kind of ornament I found out exactly one of these salespersons was wrong.

Which salesperson was wrong?

Orientation and Solution Scheme, page 48; Solution, page 106.

Outre Ornaments

ORIENTATION

The three value equivalents given must be considered in pairs to determine which one value equivalent is false. The false value equivalent leads to two derived value equivalents that are impossible; the two true value equivalents lead to one derived value equivalent that is not impossible.

SOLUTION SCHEME

Make a chart for yourself as follows:

Conditions	imply				
[1] and [2]		together with		have the same value as	
[2] and [3]					
[3] and [1]					

Complete the table with numbers of baubles, gewgaws, and trinkets.

The Widow yeah

Four women—Anna, Beth, Cass, and Dora—and three men—Earl, Fred, and Gene—play bridge, a card game for four players.

[1] The men and women consist of three married couples and a widow.

[2] The members of each married couple are never partners in a bridge game.

[3] No more than one married couple ever plays in the same bridge game.

[4] One night they played four bridge games in which the partners were as follows:

partners		partners
Anna and Earl	versus	Beth and Fred
Anna and Gene	versus	Dora and Fred
Beth and Cass	versus	Fred and Gene
Cass and Earl	versus	Dora and Gene

Who is the widow?

Solution Scheme, page 50;
Solution, page 106.

$A + F =$

BB

E F G

BG = DE

CG = DF

Cass

	E	F	G
A	X	O	X
B	X	X	x
C	X	X	o
D		X	X

AE · AG · BF · CE · BF · DF · DG

Beth

The Widow

SOLUTION SCHEME

Make a chart for yourself as follows:

	Anna	Beth	Cass	Dora
Earl				
Fred				
Gene				

Place an "X" in each of three boxes to show the three married couples that do not contradict the conditions.

Yes, Yes, Yes

Here is a list of words:

HOE   OAR   PAD   TOE   VAT

[1] Each of three logicians was told one letter of a certain word, so that each logician knew only one of the letters and so that no two logicians knew the same letter.

[2] The logicians were then told their three letters could be arranged to spell one of the words in the list above.

[3] When each logician was asked in turn "Do you know which word the letters spell?," first one logician answered "Yes," then another logician answered "Yes," and then the remaining logician answered "Yes."

Which word did the letters spell?

*Orientation and Solution
Scheme, page 52;
Solution, page 107.*

Yes, Yes, Yes

ORIENTATION

The second logician used the first logician's answer to the question to answer the question, and the third logician used the first and second logicians' answers to the question to answer the question.

SOLUTION SCHEME

Make a chart for yourself as follows:

	A	D	E	H	O	P	R	T	V
The first logician's letter may be									
The second logician's letter may be									
The third logician's letter may be									

Put a check in any column that contains a possible letter each logician may have been told—first in the top row, then in the middle row, and then in the bottom row—so that no condition is contradicted.

Hint: The first logician's letter could not be E since this would contradict [3].

Speaking of Children

"We—Aaron, Brian, and Clyde—each have some children.

[1] Aaron has at least one girl and twice as many boys as girls.

[2] Brian has at least one girl and three times as many boys as girls.

[3] Clyde has at least one girl and three more boys than girls.

[4] When I tell you the number of children we have altogether—a number less than 25—you will know how many children I have, but not how many children each of the others has. Altogether we have . . ."

Who is the speaker?

Orientation and Solution Scheme, page 54; Solution, page 108.

Speaking of Children

ORIENTATION

Some trial and error is necessary in solving this puzzle.

SOLUTION SCHEME

Make a chart for yourself as follows:

Total number of children: _____ or _____
Possible numbers of children had by:

Aaron	Brian	Clyde

Write a number in each blank and three numbers in each row of the table in as many ways as possible—crossing off any unused boxes—so that no condition is contradicted.

Mrs. Larchmont's Chair

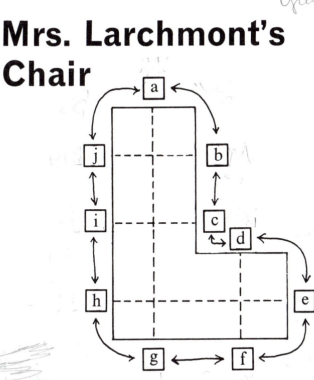

Mrs. and Mr. Larchmont invited four married couples to a dinner party. For the party, chairs were placed around an L-shaped table as shown in the diagram.

Mrs. Larchmont arranged the seating so that:

[1] Every woman sat next to her husband. (Chairs at the ends of a two-headed arrow are "next to" each other.)

(continued)

[2] Every woman sat directly across from a man. (Chairs at the ends of a dashed line are "directly across from" each other.)

[3] Mrs. Larchmont sat to the right of Mr. Larchmont.

[4] Mrs. Larchmont was the only woman who did not sit next to a woman.

In which chair—a, b, c, d, e, f, g, h, i, or j—did Mrs. Larchmont sit?

Solution Scheme, page 58;
Solution, page 109.

Card Games

Althea, Blythe, and Cheryl played some card games, each game having exactly one winner.

[1] No player won two games in succession.

[2] When a player was the dealer for a game she did not win that game.

[3] The deal proceeded from Althea to Blythe to Cheryl; then this order was repeated until they stopped playing.

[4] The only player to win more than two games did not win the first game.

Who was the only player to win more than two games?

Solution Scheme, page 59;
Solution, page 109.

Mrs. Larchmont's Chair

SOLUTION SCHEME

Make a diagram for yourself as follows:

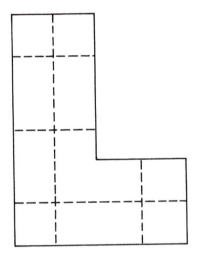

Write "X-1," "Y-1," "X-2," "Y-2," "X-3," "Y-3," "X-4," "Y-4," "X-5," or "Y-5" at each position of the table (X represents one sex, Y represents the other sex, and identical numbers indicate marriage to each other) and locate Mrs. Larchmont's chair so that no condition is contradicted.

Card Games

Make a chart for yourself as follows:

Dealer	A	B	C	A	B	C	A	B	C
Winner									

Using A, B, and C for the women, write a letter in each box —crossing off any unused boxes—so that no condition is contradicted.

Meeting Day

Lou, Moe, and Ned were at the Heave Health Club on the same day this month; it was there and then that they met.

[1] Lou, Moe, and Ned each began going to the health club last month.

[2] One of them goes every 2 days, another one goes every 3 days, and the remaining one goes every 7 days.

[3] Lou went to the health club for the first time this month on a Monday, Moe went to the health club for the first time this month on a Wednesday, and Ned went to the health club for the first time this month on a Friday.

On which day of this month did Lou, Moe, and Ned meet?

Orientation and Solution Scheme, page 62; Solution, page 110.

Meeting Day

ORIENTATION

ORIENTATION

"Day of this month" is a number from 1 through 31.

SOLUTION SCHEME

Make a chart for yourself as follows:

Health-club attendance dates this month

Lou's dates	
Moe's dates	
Ned's dates	

Write the days of this month each went to the health club so that no condition is contradicted and so that one date occurs three times.

The Tournament

Mr. and Mrs. Aye and Mr. and Mrs. Bee competed in a chess tournament. Of the three games played:

[1] In only the first game were the two players married to each other.

[2] The men won two games and the women won one game.

[3] The Ayes won more games than the Bees.

[4] Anyone who lost a game did not play a subsequent game.

Who did not lose a game?

Solution Scheme, page 64;
Solution, page 111.

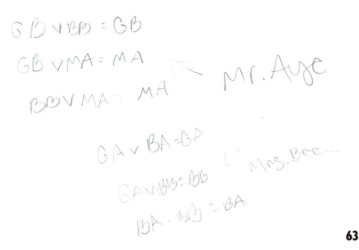

The Tournament

SOLUTION SCHEME

Make a chart for yourself as follows:

	Winner	Loser
First game		
Second game		
Third game		

Write "Mr. Aye," "Mrs. Aye," "Mr. Bee," or "Mrs. Bee" in each box so that no condition is contradicted.

Long Word

A certain word has thirteen letters.

[1] Each pair of letters below consists of one letter contained in the word and one "other" letter.

A	B	C	D	E	F	G	H	I	J	L	S	Y
V	W	Q	M	K	U	N	P	O	R	X	T	Z

[2] When the letters in the word are put in the proper order and each "other" letter is put beneath each letter in the word, the "other" letters will appear in alphabetical order.

[3] The word has the same number of letters in common with each of the following words:

FACE   QUEST   QUICK   SWITCH   WORLD

What is the word?

Orientation and Solution
Scheme, page 66;
Solution, page 112.

Long Word

Note that if Q is not the last letter in a word, it must be followed by U.

SOLUTION SCHEME

Make a chart for yourself as follows:

Ordered letters of word												
"Other" letters												

Write one letter in each box so that no condition is contradicted.

Dressing Rooms

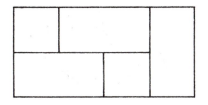

Vera, one of the performers in a play, was murdered in her dressing room. The following facts refer to the dressing rooms shown above. Each of the five performers in the play —Vera, Adam, Babe, Clay, and Dawn—had his or her own dressing room.

[1] The killer's dressing room and Vera's dressing room border on the same number of rooms.

[2] Vera's dressing room borders on Adam's dressing room and on Babe's dressing room.

[3] Clay's dressing room and Dawn's dressing room are the same size.

[4] Babe's dressing room does not border on Clay's dressing room.

Who killed Vera?

Solution Scheme, page 68;
Solution, page 114.

Dressing Rooms

Make a chart for yourself as follows:

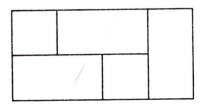

Assign each performer his or her dressing room by writing either "Adam," "Babe," "Clay," "Dawn," or "Vera" in each box so that no condition is contradicted.

Fathers and Sons

Statement A:
Both fathers always tell the truth or both fathers always lie.

Statement B:
One son always tells the truth and one son always lies.

Statement C:
Statement A and statement B are not both lies.

Of the statements above and the men who made them:

[1] Gregory made one of the statements, his father made another of the statements, and his son made the remaining statement.

[2] Each father and son mentioned in the statements refers to one of the three men.

[3] Each man either always tells the truth or always lies.

Which statement—A, B, or C—was made by Gregory?

Orientation and Solution Scheme, page 70; Solution, page 115.

Fathers and Sons

Gregory is the only one of the three who is both a father and a son.

SOLUTION SCHEME
Make a chart for yourself as follows:

Statement A	
Statement B	
Statement C	

Write "true" or "false" for each statement so that no condition is contradicted and so that the truth or falseness of each man's statement is not contradicted.

Crossing the Lake

Agnes, Becky, Cindy, and Delia crossed a lake in a canoe that held only two persons.

[1] The canoe held two persons on each of three forward trips across the lake and one person on each of two return trips.

[2] Agnes was unable to paddle when someone else was in the canoe with her.

(*continued*)

[3] Becky was unable to paddle when anyone else except Cindy was in the canoe with her.

[4] Each person paddled continuously for at least one trip.

Who paddled twice?

*Orientation and Solution
Scheme, page 74;
Solution, page 116.*

The Judge's Wife

A	1	G	7	M	13	S	19	Y	25
B	2	H	8	N	14	T	20	Z	26
C	3	I	9	O	15	U	21		
D	4	J	10	P	16	V	22		
E	5	K	11	Q	17	W	23		
F	6	L	12	R	18	X	24		

Edwin is a judge and a numerologist. He is married to a woman whose name:

[1] Has a "product" that is the same as that for JUDGE; using the correspondence of letters and numbers above, this product is $10 \times 21 \times 4 \times 7 \times 5$.

[2] Has no letter in common with JUDGE.
(To find a woman whose name satisfied the conditions above in relation to EDWIN would have been impossible.)

[3] Has no third letter of the alphabet because 3 is his unlucky number.

[4] Has its letters in alphabetical order when the first letter and the second letter are interchanged.

What is the name of the judge's wife?

Orientation and Solution Scheme, page 75; Solution, page 117.

Crossing the Lake

ORIENTATION

The situation is analogous to this simpler situation: P, Q, R, and S wish to cross a lake in a canoe that holds only two persons. So (1) P paddles Q across, (2) P paddles back, (3) P paddles R across, (4) P paddles back, (5) P paddles S across.

SOLUTION SCHEME

Make a chart for yourself as follows:

Paddler

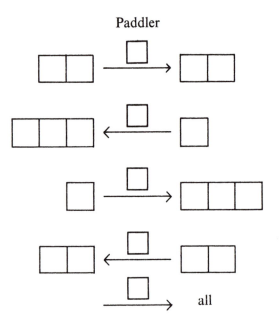

Using A, B, C, and D for the women write a letter in each box to show the paddler and the outcome of each crossing so that no condition is contradicted.

The Judge's Wife

It is not necessary to multiply the numbers to solve this puzzle; in fact, it is a good idea not to. This puzzle involves a knowledge of women's first names.

SOLUTION SCHEME

Make a chart for yourself as follows:

$10 \times 21 \times 4 \times 7 \times 5 = \_ \times \_ \times \_ \times \_ \times \_ \times \_ \times \_ \times \_ \times \_$

Write one number in each blank—crossing off any unused blanks and ×s—to indicate letters that do not contradict the conditions.

Arguments

One of four people—two men, Aubrey and Burton, and two women, Carrie and Denise—was murdered. The following facts refer to the people mentioned.

[1] Aubrey's sister argued exactly once with Carrie's legal husband after the murder.

[2] Burton's sister argued twice with the victim's legal spouse after the murder.

Who was the victim?

Orientation and Solution
Scheme, page 78;
Solution, page 118.

The Three Piles

Three piles of chips—pile I consists of one chip, pile II consists of two chips, and pile III consists of three chips—are to be used in a game played by Amelia and Beulah. The game requires:

[1] That each player in turn take only one chip or all chips from just one pile.

[2] That the player who has to take the last chip loses.

[3] That Amelia now have her turn.

From which pile should Amelia draw in order to win?

Orientation and Solution Scheme, page 79;
Solution, page 119.

Arguments

ORIENTATION

After the murder the victim could not have argued with anybody.

SOLUTION SCHEME

Make a chart for yourself as follows:

Aubrey's sister	Carrie's husband		Burton's sister	Victim's spouse

Write "Aubrey," "Burton," "Carrie," or "Denise" in each box so that no condition is contradicted.

The Three Piles

ORIENTATION

Amelia must draw from one of the piles so that, after Beulah makes any allowed draw, Amelia may draw to win eventually; on her second draw Amelia must draw so that, after Beulah makes any allowed draw, Amelia may draw to win eventually; etc. If Amelia doesn't make the one right draw each time it is her turn, Beulah gets to be in the winning position.

SOLUTION SCHEME

Make a chart for yourself as follows:

	Possible game	Possible game	Possible game
	o oo ooo	o oo ooo	o oo ooo
Amelia goes	_ __ __	_ __ __	_ __ __
Beulah goes	_ __ __	_ __ __	_ __ __
Amelia goes	_ __ __	_ __ __	_ __ __
Beulah goes	_ __ __	_ __ __	_ __ __
Amelia goes	_ __ __	_ __ __	_ __ __
Beulah goes	_ __ __	_ __ __	_ __ __

Show the chips remaining after each allowed draw so that, after any allowed draw by Beulah, Amelia can always compel Beulah to take the last chip. (Cross off any unnecessary "pile" lines.)

The Line-Up

Four men—Abraham, Barrett, Clinton, and Douglas —are standing in a line-up.

[1] One man is fair, handsome, and unscarred.

[2] Two men who are not fair are each standing next to Abraham.

[3] Barrett is the only man standing next to exactly one handsome man.

[4] Clinton is the only man not standing next to exactly one scarred man.

Who is fair, handsome, and unscarred?

Orientation and Solution Scheme, page 82; Solution, page 120.

Sum Word

```
    N O S I E R
  + A S T R A L
    7 2 5 6 1 3
```

In the addition above, the sum represents a word.

[1] Each letter represents a different digit.

[2] No letter represents zero.

What word is represented by 7 2 5 6 1 3?

Orientation and Solution Scheme, page 83; Solution, page 122.

The Line-Up

ORIENTATION

The men are standing in some order such as A B C D or C A D B. Certain orders are equivalent: for example A B C D is equivalent to D C B A; if an onlooker sees the backs of the four men while another onlooker sees their faces, the situation remains unchanged even though the order is reversed for one onlooker.

SOLUTION SCHEME

Make a chart for yourself as follows:

Fair?				
Handsome?				
Scarred?				

Write "A" (Abraham), "B" (Barrett), "C" (Clinton), and "D" (Douglas) in some order along the top of the chart and write "yes" or "no" in each box below so that no condition is contradicted.

Sum Word

ORIENTATION

Nine different letters occur in the addition, each one representing a digit other than zero (1, 2, 3, 4, 5, 6, 7, 8, and 9). Some trial and error is necessary in solving this puzzle, but the trial and error can be minimized by first considering the left two columns.

SOLUTION SCHEME

Make a chart for yourself as follows:

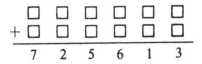

Write a digit in each box—to discover its corresponding letter—so that no condition is contradicted.

The Exam

Five students—Adele, Betty, Carol, Doris, and Ellen—answered five questions on an exam consisting of two multiple-choice (a, b, or c) questions and three true-or-false (t or f) questions.

[1] They answered the questions as follows:

	I	II	III	IV	V
Adele	a	a	t	t	t
Betty	b	b	t	f	t
Carol	a	b	t	t	f
Doris	b	c	t	t	f
Ellen	c	a	f	t	t

[2] No two students got the same number of correct answers.

Who got the most correct answers?

Orientation and Solution
Scheme, page 86;
Solution, page 123.

Sitting Ducks

Mr. and Mrs. Astor, Mr. and Mrs. Blake, Mr. and Mrs. Crane, and Mr. and Mrs. Davis were seated around a table as shown at right. At the table:

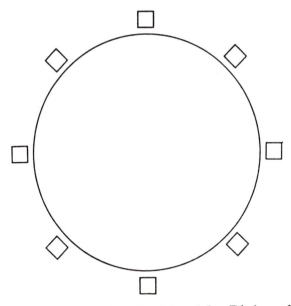

[1] Mrs. Astor was insulted by Mr. Blake who sat next to her on her left.

[2] Mr. Blake was insulted by Mrs. Crane who sat opposite him across the center of the table.

[3] Mrs. Crane was insulted by the hostess who was the only person to sit next to each one of a married couple.

[4] The hostess was insulted by the only person to sit next to each one of two men.

Who insulted the hostess?

Orientation and Solution Scheme, page 87; Solution, page 125.

The Exam

ORIENTATION

Each student has at least one true or false answer in common with every other student; knowledge of this fact eliminates much trial and error in determining the score of each student. Consideration of the total number of correct answers also eliminates much trial and error.

SOLUTION SCHEME

Make a chart for yourself as follows:

	I	II	III	IV	V
Adele	a	a	t	t	t
Betty	b	b	t	f	t
Carol	a	b	t	t	f
Doris	b	c	t	t	f
Ellen	c	a	f	t	t

Circle the correct answer to each question so that no condition is contradicted.

Sitting Ducks

ORIENTATION

The people are arranged around the table in such a way that two men are separated by one person and the members of a married couple are separated by one woman.

SOLUTION SCHEME

Make a chart for yourself as follows:

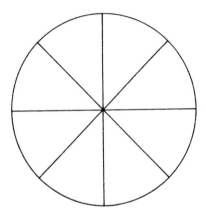

Using the symbols M_A for Astor man, W_A for Astor woman, etc., place the Astors, Blakes, Cranes, and Davises around the table so that no condition is contradicted.

The High Suit

Wilson, Xavier, Yoeman, and Zenger were playing a card game in which three cards from each player's holding remained to be played and in which one of four *suits*—clubs, diamonds, hearts, spades—was the *high suit*. The play of four cards, one from each player's holding, was a *trick*; the suit of the card played first in a trick was the *suit led*.

[1] The distribution of the four suits on the cards held by the four players was as follows:

Wilson's holding — club   heart   diamond
Xavier's holding — club   spade   spade
Yoeman's holding— club   heart   heart
Zenger's holding — spade   diamond   diamond

[2a] A player had to play a card in the suit led, if possible, at each trick.

[2b] If he could not do [2a], he had to play a card in the high suit, if possible.

[2c] If he could not do [2b], he could play any card.

[3] Each of the remaining three tricks contained in part: the suit card led, just one other card in the same suit, and a card in the high suit which won the trick.

[4] A player who won a trick had to lead at the next trick.

Which suit was the high suit?

Orientation and Solution Scheme, page 90; Solution, page 127.

The High Suit

The high suit is equivalent to the trump suit used in the play of many card games.

SOLUTION SCHEME

Make a chart for yourself as follows:

Remaining tricks	Wilson's holding	Xavier's holding	Yoeman's holding	Zenger's holding
First				
Second				
Third				

Write "C" (club), "D" (diamond), "H" (heart), or "S" (spade) in each box so that no condition is contradicted. Hint:

C	S	H	S
H	C	H	D
D	S	C	D

contradicts [2b] because clubs would be high suit (from [3]) and Yoeman's holding as given in [1] shows Yoeman would have played a heart at the first trick to a spade lead (from [3]); and contradicts [4] because clubs would be high suit and diamonds would be led at the third trick (from [3]).

Solutions

The Fight

From [1], Charles is not the older fighter. From [3], Bernard is not the younger fighter. So either:

Case I. Anthony is the older fighter and Charles is the younger fighter.

Case II. Bernard is the older fighter and Anthony is the younger fighter.

Case III. Bernard is the older fighter and Charles is the younger fighter.

Then:

From [3], Charles is the taller fighter for Case I and Charles is taller than Anthony for Case III.

From [1], Bernard is the shorter fighter for Case II and Bernard is shorter than Anthony for Case III.

From [1] and [3], Charles is taller than Bernard for Case III.

In summary:

	Older fighter	Younger fighter	Taller fighter	Shorter fighter
Case I	Anthony	Charles	Charles	Anthony
Case II	Bernard	Anthony	Anthony	Bernard
Case III	Bernard	Charles	Charles	Bernard

(Note that this reasoning eliminates nine of the twelve cases mentioned in the Discussion without considering what those nine cases are.)

From [2], Anthony is not the shorter fighter; so Case I is eliminated. From [2], Bernard cannot be both older and shorter than Charles; so Case III is eliminated. Then Case II is the correct one and *Charles is not fighting*.

Then, from [2], Bernard is younger than Charles (so Charles is the oldest of the three and Anthony is the youngest) and, from [3], Anthony is taller than Charles (so Anthony is the tallest of the three).

My Secret Word

From the "clue": If you were told any one of the letters in MOD, then you would not be able to determine whether the number of vowels in my secret word is one or two. So none of the letters in MOD is in my secret word. Then my secret word cannot be AIM, DUE, MOD, or OAT. So *my secret word is TIE.*

The Tennis Players

From [1], the players must be relatively positioned in one of the following ways:

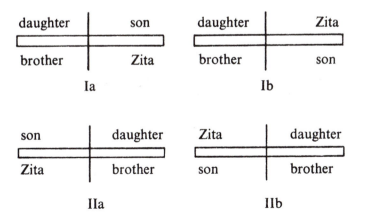

Then, from [2]: For ways Ia and IIa	For ways Ib and IIb
Brother is the worst player's sibling. Zita is the worst player.	Daughter is the worst player's sibling. Son is the worst player.

Then, from [3]: For ways Ia and IIa	For ways Ib and IIb
Brother is the best player.	Brother is the best player.

So, in any case, *Zita's brother is the best player.*

After-Dinner Drink

From [1] and [2] there are six possibilities:

	Abigail orders	Bridget orders	Claudia orders
Case I	coffee	coffee	coffee
Case II	coffee	tea	tea
Case III	tea	coffee	coffee
Case IV	tea	tea	tea
Case V	tea	coffee	tea
Case VI	tea	tea	coffee

Then, from [3], Cases I and V are eliminated and, from [4], Cases II and V are eliminated. So you know *Abigail always orders the same drink* (tea) *after dinner.*

Equal Sums

One digit must be 9. Then, from [1] and [2], 9 must go with 1 and 3. One digit must be 8. Then, from [1] and [2], 8 must go with either·1 and 4 or 2 and 3. One digit must be 7. Then, from [1] and [2], 7 must go with either 1 and 5 or 2 and 4. One digit must be 6. Then, from [1] and [2], 6 must go with either 2 and 5 or 3 and 4.

From the diagram no digit may be used in more than two sums. From this and the fact that 9 goes with 1 and 3:

Case I. If 8 goes with 1 and 4, then 7 goes with 2 and 4; then 6 goes with 2 and 5.

Case II. If 8 goes with 2 and 3, then 6 goes with 2 and 5; then 7 goes with 1 and 5.

But Case II is impossible because the digit 4 does not occur. So Case I is correct and, from the diagram, *E must be 4*.

A possible arrangement of the digits is shown below.

```
9 3 1
  8
  4 7 2
    5
    6
```

Relations

From [1]:

If Lee's spouse is Dale, then Dale's sibling cannot be Lee and must be Terry; then Terry's sister-in-law cannot be Dale and must be Lee.

If Lee's spouse is Terry, then Terry's sister-in-law cannot

be Lee and must be Dale; then Dale's sibling cannot be Terry and must be Lee.

Then, in any case, all three of Lee, Dale, and Terry are accounted for and Terry's sister-in-law is a female.

So, from [2], Lee's spouse and Dale's sibling are both males. In summary:

	Lee's spouse	Dale's sibling	Terry's sister-in-law
	male	male	female
Case I	Dale	Terry	Lee
Case II	Terry	Lee	Dale

Case II is eliminated because Lee and Terry cannot both be males and married to each other. So Case I is the correct one and you know *Dale is a married man.* Lee is a married woman, Dale and Terry are brothers, and Lee is Terry's sister-in-law.

1	2	3
4	5	6
7	8	9

X and O

Let a number in each square as shown indicate the location of a mark. Then, from [3], the seventh mark must be placed in square 5 and, from [2], the seventh mark wins for both X and O. So the sixth mark must have been placed in a line already containing two of the opponent's marks—in either square 7 or square 9; otherwise, either X or O would have been placed in square 5. But, from [3], the sixth mark could not have been placed in square 7 because square 5 would have been the required location for the O in square 7. So the sixth mark was placed in square 9 and was X. Then, from [1], the seventh mark will be O and, from [2], *O wins the game.*

From previous reasoning, the fifth mark placed in the game can also be determined: O in square 8.

Names

From [1] and [4], Miss Alden, Miss Brent, and Miss Clark are named Fay. From [1], no one can have more than two of the names; so, from [1] and [2], Kay is distributed only twice with Fay in one of two ways:

Case I   Alden Brent Clark Doyle Evans

                      Fay   Fay   Fay

                      Kay   Kay

Case II   Alden Brent Clark Doyle Evans

                      Fay   Fay   Fay

                                Kay   Kay

Then, from [1] and [3], neither Miss Brent nor Miss Clark is named Gay in either case. So—from [1]—Miss Alden, Miss Doyle, and Miss Evans are named Gay. Then Case I is impossible and Case II becomes:

Case II   Alden Brent Clark Doyle Evans

                      Fay   Fay   Fay

                                Kay   Kay

                      Gay   Gay   Gay

Then, from [1], Miss Evans is named Fay. Then, from [1], *Miss Brent is named May.*

Hockey Scores

From [1] and [3]: The team that lost the greatest number of games lost the two games it played (there were three losers and the teams could not have each lost one game). So the team that lost the greatest number of games did not score 6 and did not score 5 and 4 together. The highest total of two scores achieved by this team is greater than the total of at least 7 (6 and at least 1) achieved by some other team. So this team scored 5 and 3 for a total of 8.

Then the 5 score lost to the 6 score and the 3 score lost to the 4 score. So the 1 score and the 2 score go together and the 6 and the 1 were scored by the same team. Let the teams be X, Y, and Z temporarily; then in summary:

Z	Y
1	2

X	Y
3	4

X	Z
5	6

From inspection of the team scores, any two higher scores differ by at least one and at most two; any two lower scores differ by at least one and at most two. So, from [2], the Angoras' higher score and the Bobcats' higher score differ by two and the Bobcats' lower score and the Cougars' lower score differ by one. So the Angoras must be Z, the Bobcats must be Y, and the Cougars must be X. Then *the Cougars achieved the highest total of its two scores.*

The Journey

From [3]: No two of the L-shaped fields are the same kind of field; these can be assigned letters, such as east-E, west-W, and south-S, to represent either corn, wheat, or rye. Then E, W, and S can be assigned to the fields surrounding them by alternating W and S around the east L-shaped field, alternating E and S around the west L-shaped field, and alternating E and W around the south L-shaped field. Then 1 is a W field, 5 is an E field, and 12 is an S field.

1W		4	5 E	
2 E	3S	W	6 S	
W		east		
west		E	10W	
		south		
7	8	9	S	11	12
S	E	W		E	S

From [1] and [2] and inspection of the plan, the only possible route involves fields 6-S, 4-W, 3-S, west L-shaped, south L-shaped, 10-W, and 12-S. So, from [2], each E field is a rye field and *the east L-shaped field is a rye field*.

The Visits

From [1] and any of [2], [3], and [4], at least one woman visited Edna in the morning and at least one woman visited Edna in the evening. From [3], Alma did not visit Edna first. So, from [1], the order of the visits must be one of the following:

Case I.   Bess (9), Alma (8), Cleo (10), Dina (11)
Case II.   Bess (9), Cleo (10), Alma (8), Dina (11)
Case III. Bess (9), Cleo (10), Dina (11), Alma (8)
Case IV.   Bess (9), Dina (11), Alma (8), Cleo (10)
Case V.   Cleo (10), Alma (8), Bess (9), Dina (11)
Case VI.   Cleo (10), Dina (11), Alma (8), Bess (9)
Case VII. Dina (11), Alma (8), Bess (9), Cleo (10)

From [2], Cases I, V, VI, and VII are eliminated. Then, from [4], Cases II and III are eliminated. So Case IV is the right one and *Cleo visited Edna last.*

A Different Age

Let W, X, Y, and Z represent the four digits as shown in the diagram. Then, from [1] and [2], Ambrose's age is a two-digit number and WX plus Brandon's age equals WY. So Brandon's age must be a one-digit number.

From [3], WY plus Chester's age equals ZY. So Chester's age must end in zero. Then Chester's age must be a two-digit number.

From [4] and the fact that only Brandon's age is a one-digit number, *Brandon is a different age in years from the other two.*

Because Chester's age ends in zero, Ambrose's age must end in zero. So Ambrose and Chester may each be 10, 20, 30, or 40 and Brandon may be 1, 2, 3, 4, 5, 6, 7, 8, or 9. Of the thirty-six possible ways to complete the diagram, here is one:

The Doctor and the Lawyer

The two women are not blood relatives. So, from [2], if the doctor is a woman, the lawyer is a man. Then, from [3], the doctor is a man. Because a contradiction arises from assuming the doctor is a woman, the doctor must be a man.

Mr. Horton's son is the youngest of the four and is a blood relative of each of the other three. So, from [1], the doctor is not Mr. Horton's son. Then *you know the occupation of Mr. Horton: he is the doctor.*

From [1], then, the lawyer cannot be Mr. Horton's mother. So the lawyer is either his wife or his son. (The doctor may be older than the lawyer.) Then *you don't know the occupation of anyone else.*

The Two Cubes

From [1] and the pictured cubes, at least one of ● and ■ occurs twice.

If both occur twice, then the identical cubes look like:

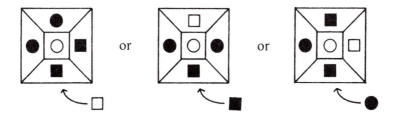

But in each case duplicate faces cannot occur at the arrows, contradicting [2].

So either only ● occurs twice or only ■ occurs twice.

If only ● occurs twice, then the identical cubes look like this:

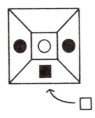

But in this case duplicate faces cannot occur at the arrows, contradicting [2].

So only ■ occurs twice and the identical cubes look like this:

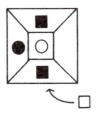

In this case the ○ occurs on the right cube at the arrow. So, from [2], the ○ occurs on the left cube at the arrow. Thus ○ *is on the faces indicated by the arrows*. (The ○ occurs on the unmarked face in the last diagram.)

The Guards

From [1] and [2], Ida stands guard on only two days each week. Then in [4] Ida is not one of the unknown guards and either Bob (Case I) or Cab (Case II) stands guard with Art on Wednesday.

So, using this information and [3] to complete [4] in each case:

Case I. If Bob stands guard on Wednesday, then Art stands guard on Friday. Then Cab stands guard on Thursday and Bob stands guard on Saturday. Then Art stands guard on Monday. Then Cab stands guard on Tuesday.

Case II. If Cab stands guard on Wednesday, then Art stands guard on Thursday. Then Bob stands guard on Tuesday and Friday. Then Art stands guard on Monday. Then Cab stands guard on Saturday.

In either case, *Art does not stand guard with Ida.*

Brothers

From [4], six cases are possible:

	Eye color of Amos	Eye color of Bert	Eye color of Clem
Case I	hazel	blue	
Case II	hazel		blue
Case III	blue	hazel	
Case IV		hazel	blue
Case V	blue		hazel
Case VI		blue	hazel

From [1], then, a fourth brother has grey eyes in each case. Then: from [1] and [2], Cases I and VI are impossible; from [1] and [3], Cases II and IV are impossible; from [1] and [3], Clem has grey eyes in Case III; and, from [1] and [2], Bert has grey eyes in Case V.

So *you know only the color of Amos' eyes: they are blue.* (Any more than four brothers must also have blue eyes, from [3].)

Equal Products

From [1] and [2]: No letter can be 0, 5, or 7. The product for each row, then, is a multiple of 1, 2, 3, 4, 6, 8, and 9. So the smallest possible product is 8×9 or 72 and the product is a multiple of 72. But the product cannot be any of 72×2, 72×3, etc. because it is not possible to get a product larger than 72 three times. So the product is 72.

Then:

$$72 = \boxed{1 \times 8 \times 9} = 2 \times 36$$
$$= \boxed{2 \times 4 \times 9} = 3 \times 24$$
$$= \boxed{3 \times 4 \times 6}$$

Because 4 and 9 are used twice (see boxed products), B or E is 4 and the other is 9. So *G is 2*.

A possible arrangement of digits is:

$$
\begin{array}{ccc}
6 & & 8 \\
4 & 2 & 9 \\
3 & & 1
\end{array}
$$

Tees and Els

From [1] and [2]:

Case I. If Annette's statement is true, all three cannot be members of the Tee family and Cynthia cannot be the only one of the three who is a member of the El family. So, if Annette's statement is true, either: Annette is the only one of the three who is a member of the Tee family or Bernice is the only one of the three who is a member of the El family.

Case II. If Annette's statement is false, Annette cannot be the only one of the three who is a member of the El family and Bernice cannot be the only one of the three who is a member of the Tee family. So, if Annette's statement is false, either: Cynthia is the only one of the three who is a member of the Tee family or all three are members of the El family.

Then: Annette is a member of the Tee family in Case I and Annette is a member of the El family in Case II. Bernice is a member of the El family in Case I and Bernice is a member of the El family in Case II. Cynthia may be a member of either family in Case I and Cynthia may be a member of either family in Case II. So *you know only the name of Bernice's family* (El).

The Joker

From [1] and [3], one man had exactly two singletons: a king and a queen. From [2], Bill cannot have had exactly two singletons. From [1] and [2], Carl cannot have had exactly two singletons unless one of them was the joker. So Alec had the singleton king and the singleton queen.

Then, from [3], each of Bill and Carl cannot have had more than one singleton. If Carl had no singletons, then—from Alec's holding and [1] and [2]—he had two kings and two queens. But then, from [1] and [2], Bill would have had three singletons—contradicting previous reasoning. So Carl had exactly one singleton.

Then—from [1], [2], and [4]—Carl had three queens and a singleton king; if Carl had the joker instead of a singleton king, Bill would have had three kings—contradicting [4]. Then, from the other men's holdings and from [1] and [2], *Bill had the joker* and two kings.

Outre Ornaments

Let b represent baubles, g represent gewgaws, t represent trinkets, + represent "together with," and = represent "have the same value as." Using [2], substitute 4b+9t for 5g in [1]. Using [3], substitute 6t+3g for 4b in [2]. Using [1], substitute 7b+5g for 6t in [3]. Then simplify. In summary:

	Using [2]		Simplify	
[1] 7b+5g=6t	$\longrightarrow$	7b+4b+9t=6t	$\longrightarrow$	11b+9t=6t

	Using [3]		Simplify	
[2] 4b+9t=5g	$\longrightarrow$	6t+3g+9t=5g	$\longrightarrow$	15t+3g=5g

	Using [1]		Simplify	
[3] 6t+3g=4b	$\longrightarrow$	7b+5g+3g=4b	$\longrightarrow$	7b+8g=4b

[1], using [2], is impossible because some baubles and 9 trinkets cannot have the same value as 6 trinkets. [3], using [1], is impossible because some gewgaws and 7 baubles cannot have the same value as 4 baubles. Because only one salesperson was wrong, from [4], neither the second nor the third salesperson was wrong; otherwise, more than one salesperson was wrong. So only *the first salesperson was wrong.*

One possible price list, from [2] and [3], is:
trinket—$ .80
bauble—$5.70
gewgaw—$6.00

The Widow

From [1], [2], and [4]:
Either Fred is married to Anna or Fred is married to Cass.
If Fred is married to Anna, then Gene is married to Beth or Gene is married to Cass.

If Gene is married to Beth, then Earl is married to Dora.

If Gene is married to Cass, then Earl is married to Beth or Earl is married to Dora.

If Fred is married to Cass, then Gene is married to Beth; then Earl is married to Dora.

In summary, the married couples are either:

Case I		Case II		Case III		Case IV
Fred-Anna		Fred-Anna*		Fred-Anna		Fred-Cass*
Gene-Beth	or	Gene-Cass	or	Gene-Cass*	or	Gene-Beth*
Earl-Dora		Earl-Beth*		Earl-Dora*		Earl-Dora

From [3] and [4], Cases II, III, and IV are impossible (asterisks show two couples in one game). So Case I is the correct one and, from [1], *Cass is the widow.*

Yes, Yes, Yes

From [1], [2], and [3]: The first logician to answer "Yes" must have been told a letter that occurred only once in the list. So the first logician was told either H, R, P, D, or V. Then the second logician knew the first logician was told either H, R, P, D, or V. So the second logician knew the word was not TOE. Then the second logician knew what the word was if told T or E (some new letter), or if told the second letter of PAD that occurred only once in the list: P or D. The third logician knew the first logician was told either H, R, P, D, or V and knew the second logician was told either T, E, P, or D. So the third logician knew the word was not OAR. So the third logician knew what the word was if told O (some new letter), but would not know what the word was if told A. Then, rather than PAD or VAT, *the letters spelled HOE.*

Speaking of Children

From [1], Aaron has at least 3 children and a number of children from this sequence: 3, 6, 9, 12, 15...

From [2], Brian has at least 4 children and a number of children from this sequence: 4, 8, 12, 16...

From [3], Clyde has at least 5 children and a number of children from this sequence: 5, 7, 9, 11, 13, 15, 17...

Then the total number of children is at least 12 and, from [4], at most 24. Also: If the total number of children is even, Aaron must have an odd number of children; if the total number of children is odd, Aaron must have an even number of children.

Trial and error reveals the following information. The total number of children cannot be 13 because no three numbers, one from each sequence, can total 13. The total cannot be 12, 14, 15, or 17 because the number of children each had would be known, contradicting [4]. The total cannot be 18, 20, 21, 22, 23, or 24 because then no number of children could be known for anybody, contradicting [4]. So the total is 16 or 19.

Case I. When the total is 16 Aaron must have an odd number of children and, from the sequences, this number must not be greater than 16 – (4 + 5) or 7. So Aaron must have 3 children.

Case II. When the total is 19 Aaron must have an even number of children and, from the sequences, this number must not be greater than 19 – (4 + 5) or 10. So Aaron must have 6 children.

Then, in each case, Brian and Clyde together must have 13 children. Then Brian must have either 4 or 8 children. Then: If Brian has 4 children, Clyde has 9 children; if Brian has 8 children, Clyde has 5 children.

So, in any case, *the speaker is Aaron.*

Mrs. Larchmont's Chair

Let X represent one sex, let Y represent the other sex, and place an X in chair a.

Then, from [1], the spouse of the person in chair a is either in chair b—Case I—or in chair j—Case II. Conditions [1] and [2] can be used alternately to determine the couples (X-1 and Y-1, X-2 and Y-2, etc.) in each case, by beginning at chair a and following the arrows:

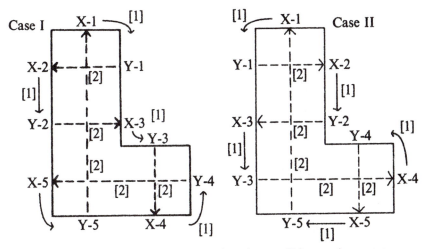

In Case I, three members of each sex did not sit next to a member of the same sex; so, from [4], Case I is eliminated. Then Case II is the correct case.

Then, from [4], Mrs. Larchmont sat in either chair i or chair j. Then, from [3], *Mrs. Larchmont sat in chair j.*

Card Games

Let A represent Althea, B represent Blythe, and C represent Cheryl. Then, from [1] and [2], the possible sequence of wins is as follows:

Dealers, from [3]	A	B	C	A	B	C	A	B
Case I	C*	A	B	C	A	B	C	–
Case II	B	A*	B	C	A	B	–	–
Case III	B	C	B*	C	A	B	–	–
Case IV	B	C	A	C*	A	B	C	–
Case V	B	C	A	B	A*	B	–	–
Case VI	B	C	A	B	C	B*	–	–
Case VII	B	C	A	B	C	A	C*	–
Case VIII	B	C	A	B	C	A	B	–

From [4], listing continues until one player wins three games. (Each asterisk indicates the point where the rest of a sequence is determined; one deal earlier a choice between two players is possible. Each succeeding case represents the other choice for the preceding case.) From [4], Cases I, II, III, V, VI, and VIII are eliminated. So Case IV or VII is the right one. In either case, *Cheryl was the only player to win more than two games.*

Meeting Day

From [1] and [2], the two-day man went to the health club for the first time this month on the 1st or the 2nd and the three-day man went to the health club for the first time this month on the 1st, 2nd, or 3rd. Then, from [3], the two-day man went on the 1st and the three-day man went on the 3rd. Then—from [1], [2], and [3]—the seven-day man went to the health club for the first time this month on either the 5th or the 6th. In summary, either A or B below is true.

A. Lou went on Monday, the 1st, and every two days thereafter; Moe went on Wednesday, the 3rd, and every three days thereafter; and Ned went on Friday, the 5th, and every seven days thereafter.

B. Moe went on Wednesday, the 1st, and every two days thereafter; Ned went on Friday, the 3rd, and every three days thereafter; and Lou went on Monday, the 6th, and every seven days thereafter.

The dates for A and B, then, are as follows (the dates in parentheses depend upon the length of the month):

A. Lou's dates—1, 3, 5, 7, 9, 11, 13, 15, 17, 19, 21, 23, 25, 27, (29), (31)
Moe's dates—3, 6, 9, 12, 15, 18, 21, 24, 27, (30)
Ned's dates—5, 12, 19, 26

B. Moe's dates—1, 3, 5, 7, 9, 11, 13, 15, 17, 19, 21, 23, 25, 27, (29), (31)
Ned's dates—3, 6, 9, 12, 15, 18, 21, 24, 27, (30)
Lou's dates—6, 13, 20, 27

Because the three men were at the health club on the same day this month, possibility A is eliminated. So possibility B is correct. Possibility B reveals that *Lou, Moe, and Ned met on the 27th of this month.*

The Tournament

From [2] and [3], either:

I. Mr. Aye won one game, Mrs. Aye won one game, and Mr. Bee won one game; or
II. Mr. Aye won two games and Mrs. Aye won one game; or
III. Mr. Aye won two games and Mrs. Bee won one game.

If I is correct, then: From [1] and [4], Mr. Bee beat Mrs. Bee in the first game. Then, from [4], only Mr. Bee could have lost to Mr. Aye or Mrs. Aye in the second game. Then, from [1] and [4], no one could have played against the last winner in the last game. So I is not correct.

II cannot be correct from [1] and [4].

So III is correct. If Mrs. Bee won the first game, then she beat Mr. Bee in that game, from [1]. But then, from [1] and [4], no one could have played against Mr. Aye in the second game. So Mr. Aye won the first game against Mrs. Aye, from [1]. Then, from [4], Mr. Aye beat Mr. Bee in the second game. Then, from [4], Mrs. Bee beat Mr. Aye in the third game.

So *only Mrs. Bee did not lose a game.*

Long Word

From [3], the number of common letters is at most four. From [1] and QUEST in [3], the number of common letters is at least one—S or T. From [1], from FACE and QUEST in [3], and from the fact that Q cannot occur in the thirteen-letter word without U:

	If the number of common letters is	then each of these loops contains a common letter	then each of these loops contains a common letter
(i)	4	(Q)(U)(E) S T C F K T S	F A C (E) (U) V (Q) K
(ii)	1	Q U E S T (C)(F)(K) T S	(F) A (C) E U V Q (K)
(iii)	2	Q (U) E S T (C) F (K) T S	F A (C) E (U) V Q (K)
(iv)	2	Q U (E) S T (C)(F) K T S	(F) A (C)(E) U V Q K

or

112

(v)	3	Q U E S T C F K T S	F A C E U V Q K

or

(vi)	3	Q U E S T C F K T S	F A C E U V Q K

A contradiction occurs in (i), (ii), (iv), and (v), so these are eliminated.

Then, from (iii) and (vi), A is a common letter.

Then, from [1] and from QUICK in [3]:

	If each of these loops contains a common letter	then each of these loops contains a common letter	Possible?
(iii)	Q U E S T F A C E C F K T S U V Q K	Q U I C K C F O Q E	no
(vi)	Q U E S T F A C E C F K T S U V Q K	Q U I C K C F O Q E	yes

Then I is the third common letter in QUICK.

Then, from [1] and [3], the common letters in SWITCH are I, C, and S/T. Then, from [1] and [3], the common letters in WORLD are not W and not O (because I is common); so the common letters in WORLD are R, L, and D.

Ten of the thirteen letters are now known: C, U, E, A, I, R, L, D, P (not H), and B (not W). So, from [1] and [2], twenty-four letters can be arranged thus (the pairs S/T and Y/Z can only go where indicated):

UP RE D I C S A B L Y
F H J K M O Q T V W X Z

It is now easy to see that: the letters in the pair G/N should be reversed and placed after the pair U/F, the letters in the pair S/T should be reversed, and *the word is UNPREDICTABLY.*

Dressing Rooms

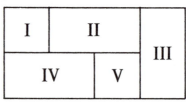

From [4], neither Babe nor Clay occupies dressing room II; from [1], Vera does not occupy dressing room II. So either Adam or Dawn occupies dressing room II.

Suppose Adam occupies dressing room II; then, from [3], one of the following sets of occupation must exist (A represents Adam, C represents Clay, and D represents Dawn):

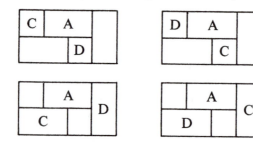

But, from [2], each of these sets of occupation is impossible.

So Dawn occupies dressing room II. Then, from [3], one of the following sets of occupation must exist:

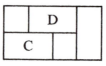

But, from [2], the first of these sets is impossible. So the second set is the correct one and, from [2], Vera occupies dressing room IV.

Then, from [4], Babe occupies dressing room I. So Adam occupies dressing room V.

Then, from [1], *Adam killed Vera.*

Fathers and Sons

If statement C is false, statement A and statement B are both false. But—from [1], [2], and [3]—if statement A is false, statement B or statement C is true (because a false statement A implies one father always tells the truth and one father always lies). So statement C cannot be false and must be true.

Because statement C is true, at least one of statements A and B is true. But—from [1] and [2]—if statement B is true, statement A or statement C is false. So if statement B is true, statement A is false.

In summary:

	Case I	Case II
Statement A	true	false
Statement B	false	true
Statement C	true	true

If Case I were the right one, then—from statement A and from [2]—the speakers of statements A and C would both be fathers; and—from statement B and from [2] and [3]—the speakers of statements A and C would both be sons (because a false statement B implies both sons always tell the truth or both sons always lie). This situation is impossible from [1] because only Gregory is both a father and a son; so Case I is eliminated.

Then Case II is the right one. Then, from statement A and

from [2] and [3], the speaker of statement A is a father; and, from statement B and from [2], the speaker of statement A is a son. So, from [1], *Gregory made statement A.*

Crossing the Lake

From [1], [2], and [4], Agnes paddled on at least one return trip.

The person who paddled twice did not paddle on two forward trips because, from [1], she would then have had to paddle on a return trip, contradicting [4]. So the person who paddled twice paddled on at least one return trip.

In summary, Agnes and the person who paddled twice each paddled on at least one return trip. So Becky, Cindy, and Delia each paddled on one forward trip, from [1] and [4].

Then, from [1] and [3], Cindy was in the canoe when Becky paddled on a forward trip. Because Cindy was in the canoe on two forward trips, she must have paddled on a return trip. So *Cindy paddled twice.*

Six paddling sequences are possible. To determine an actual sequence of paddlings, Celia's (C) and Agnes' (A) paddlings are listed first, then Becky's (B) paddling, and then Delia's (D) paddling. The sequences are shown below.

C	D	D
BD ⟶ AC	BC ⟶ AD	BC ⟶ AD
A	A	A
ABD ⟵ C	ABC ⟵ D	ABC ⟵ D
D	C	B
B ⟶ ACD	B ⟶ ACD	A ⟶ BCD
C	C	C
BC ⟵ AD	BC ⟵ AD	AC ⟵ BD
B	B	C
⟶ all	⟶ all	⟶ all

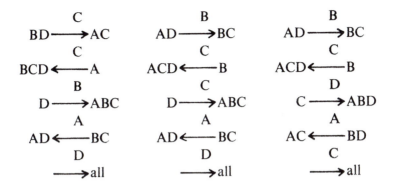

The Judge's Wife

From [1], the name of the judge's wife has a "product" of

$$10 \times 21 \times 4 \times 7 \times 5.$$

From [2], her name has no G(7) or U(21); so it has N(14) twice. Division by 14 twice leaves $10 \times 3 \times 5$.

$$
\begin{array}{r|l}
14 & 10 \times 21 \times 4 \times 7 \times 5 \\
14 & 10 \times 21 \times 2 \times 5 \\
\hline
 & 10 \times 3 \times 5
\end{array}
$$

From [2], her name has no E(5) or J(10). It cannot have a T(20). It cannot have an O(15); otherwise, it would have an E(5) or a J(10). So her name has a Y(25). Division by 25 leaves 2×3.

$$
\begin{array}{r|l}
25 & 10 \times 3 \times 5 \\
\hline
 & 2 \times 3
\end{array}
$$

From [3], her name has an F(6). Division by 6 leaves 1.

$$
\begin{array}{r|l}
6 & 2 \times 3 \\
\hline
 & 1
\end{array}
$$

In alphabetical order the letters found so far are FNNY and the only other letter her name may contain is A(1). So, from [4], *the name of the judge's wife is FANNY*.

(The W in Edwin is the twenty-third letter of the alphabet and can only be represented as 23×1. So to find a woman whose name satisfied the first two conditions in relation to EDWIN is impossible.)

Arguments

From [1], Aubrey's sister is either Carrie or Denise.

Suppose Aubrey's sister is Carrie. Then, from [1], Carrie's husband is Burton. Then, from [1] and [2], Burton's sister is Denise.

Suppose Aubrey's sister is Denise. Then, from [1], Carrie's husband is either Aubrey or Burton. Suppose Carrie's husband is Aubrey; then, from [2], Burton's sister can be either Carrie or Denise. Suppose Carrie's husband is Burton; then, from [1] and [2], Burton's sister is Denise.

In summary:

	Arguers in [1]		Arguers in [2]	
	Aubrey's sister	Carrie's husband	Burton's sister	Victim's spouse
Case I.	Carrie	Burton	Denise	?
Case IIa.	Denise	Aubrey	Carrie	?
Case IIb.	Denise	Aubrey	Denise	?
Case IIc.	Denise	Burton	Denise	?

In Case I, Aubrey must be the victim. Then the victim's legal spouse can only be Denise. This situation is impossible, so Case I is eliminated.

In Case IIb, either Burton or Carrie must be the victim. If Burton is the victim, then Burton can have no legal spouse;

this situation contradicts [2]. If Carrie is the victim, then Denise and Aubrey argued exactly once—from [1]—and twice—from [2]; this situation is impossible. So Case IIb is eliminated.

In Case IIc, either Aubrey or Carrie must be the victim. If Aubrey is the victim, then Aubrey can have no legal spouse; this situation contradicts [2]. If Carrie is the victim, then Denise and Burton argued exactly once—from [1]—and twice—from [2]; this situation is impossible. So Case IIc is eliminated.

Then Case IIa is the correct one. Then *Burton must be the victim*. From [2], Burton's spouse can only be Denise.

The Three Piles

In the chart below:

For the first four opening moves by Amelia, only winning moves by Beulah are given for any moves by Amelia after the opening.

For the last opening move by Amelia, any moves by Beulah are given for only winning moves by Amelia.

When two piles have the same number of chips, a removal of some chips from one pile is equivalent to a removal of the same number of chips from the other pile.

From [1] and [3]:	Amelia takes pile III	Amelia takes pile II
From [1]: { Amelia goes / Beulah goes / Amelia goes	O ___ OO ___ O ___ ___ ___ ___ ___ ___	O ___ ___ OOO O ___ ___ ___ ___ ___ ___
From [2]:	Amelia loses	Amelia loses

119

From [1] and [3]:	Amelia takes pile I	Amelia takes one chip from pile III
From [1]: Amelia goes	___ OO OOO	O __ OO OO
Beulah goes	___ OO OO	___ OO OO
Amelia goes	___ O OO	___ OO ___
Beulah goes	___ O ___	___ O ___
Amelia goes	___ ___ ___	___ ___ ___
From [2]:	Amelia loses	Amelia loses

From [1] and [3]:	Amelia takes one chip from pile II		
From [1]: Amelia goes	O __ O OOO	O __ O OOO	O __ O OOO
Beulah goes	___ O OOO	O __ O OO	O __ O ___
Amelia goes	___ O ___	O __ O O	___ O ___
Beulah goes	___ ___ ___	___ O O	___ ___ ___
Amelia goes	___ ___ ___	___ O ___	___ ___ ___
Beulah goes	___ ___ ___	___ ___ ___	___ ___ ___
From [2]:	Amelia wins	Amelia wins	Amelia wins

So *Amelia should draw one chip from pile II in order to win.*

The Line-Up

From [2] (A represents Abraham and ? represents an unknown man):

Fair ? | ? | A | ? |
        | no | | no |

So, from [1], either:

	?	A	?	?
Fair?	no	yes	no	
Handsome?		yes		
Scarred?		no		

Case I

or

	?	A	?	?
Fair?	no		no	yes
Handsome?				yes
Scarred?				no

Case II

Each of two scarred men cannot be standing next to Clinton in either Case I or Case II. So, from [4], Clinton is standing next to no scarred man and each of the other men is standing next to exactly one scarred man. Then either (C represents Clinton):

	C	A	?	?
Fair?	no	yes	no	
Handsome?		yes		
Scarred?	no	no	yes	yes

Case I

or

	?	A	?	C
Fair?	no		no	yes
Handsome?				yes
Scarred?	yes	yes	no	no

Case II

In Case I, Clinton is standing next to exactly one handsome man. So, from [3], Case I is impossible.

Then Case II is the correct one and *only Clinton is fair, handsome, and unscarred.*

In Case II, the man next to Clinton cannot be handsome, from [3]. Then, from [3], the man on the other end from Clinton cannot be handsome. If Abraham is handsome, Barrett is on the other end (from [3]). If Abraham is not handsome, Barrett is standing next to Clinton (from [3]). So either (B represents Barrett and D represents Douglas):

	B	A	D	C
Fair?	no		no	yes
Handsome?	no	yes	no	yes
Scarred?	yes	yes	no	no

Case IIa

or

	D	A	B	C
Fair?	no		no	yes
Handsome?	no	no	no	yes
Scarred?	yes	yes	no	no

Case IIb

Abraham may be either fair or not fair.

Sum Word

N+A cannot be 7; otherwise, O and S are both 1 which contradicts [1] or one of O and S is zero which contradicts [2]. So N+A is 6 and 1 is carried from O+S. Then, from [1] and [2], the possible digits for N and A are as follows:

N	5	1	4	2
A	1	5	2	4

Then R+L cannot be 3; otherwise, R and L are 3 and 0, which contradicts [2], or 1 and 2, which contradicts [1]. So R+L is 13.

Then E+A is 10.

So, choosing values for R and L from [1], the table can be continued:

	i	ii	iii	iv	v	vi	vii
N	5	5	1	4	4	2	2
A	1	1	5	2	2	4	4
E	9	9	–	8	8	6	6
L	7	6		7	6	8	5
R	6	7		6	7	5	8

Case iii is eliminated from [1].

Then R+I is 15 and not 5, from [2]. So, from [2], Case vi is eliminated and, from [1], Cases i and v are eliminated.

Then continuing the table:

	ii	iv	vii
N	5	4	2
A	1	2	4
E	9	8	6
L	6	7	5
R	7	6	8
I	8	9	7

Then S+T is 4 and not 14, from [1]. So, from [1] and [2], Case ii is eliminated and O+S is 12. Then continuing the table:

	iv	iv	vii	vii
N	4	4	2	2
A	2	2	4	4
E	8	8	6	6
L	7	7	5	5
R	6	6	8	8
I	9	9	7	7
T	3	1	3	1
S	1	3	1	3
O	–	–	–	9

Case iv is eliminated from [1].

So Case vii is the correct one. Substituting the letters for the digits, *7 2 5 6 1 3 is I N L E T S.*

The Exam

From [1], each student has at least one true-false answer in common with every other student. So if one student got five correct answers, then each student got at least one correct answer. Then, from [2], the number of correct answers must total 1+2+3+4+5 or 15. Because the maximum number of correct answers is 2 (a or b) +2 (a or b) +4 (t) +4 (t) +3 (t) or 15, from [1], Adele's answers would have to be the five correct ones. But then Betty and Doris would each have exactly two correct answers, and Carol and Ellen would each have exactly three correct answers, contradicting [2]. So no one got five correct answers.

Then, from [2], the number of correct answers must total 0+1+2+3+4 or 10. Then the student who got none correct cannot be Adele, Carol, or Doris because the total number of correct answers cannot be the required 10 when the correct answers for III and IV are both f; because each f occurs only once, the maximum total possible would be 9. So Betty or Ellen got none correct.

If Betty got none correct, then the correct answers for the true-false questions would be: III. f (occurs once), IV. t (occurs four times), and V. f (occurs twice). Then Carol, Doris, and Ellen would each have at least two correct answers; so Adele would have to be the student with one correct answer: IV. t (occurs four times). Adele's and Betty's multiple-choice answers would, then, be incorrect; so the correct multiple-choice answers would have to be: I. c (occurs once) and II. c (occurs once). But, then, the total number of correct answers would not be the required 10: 1 (c) +1 (c) +1 (f) +4 (t) +2 (f) =9. So it is Ellen and not Betty who got no correct answers.

Because Ellen got none correct, the correct answers for the true-false questions must be: III. t (occurs four times), IV. f (occurs once), and V. f (occurs twice). Then Betty, Carol, and Doris each got at least two correct answers; so Adele got one correct answer: III. t (occurs four times). Then Adele's and Ellen's multiple-choice answers are incorrect; so the correct multiple-choice answer for I is b (occurs twice); so, because the total number of correct answers is 10, the correct multiple-choice answer for II must be c (occurs once).

In summary, the correct answers in order are: b, c, t, f, f and are shown below in circles.

	I	II	III	IV	V
Adele	a	a	ⓣ	t	t
Betty	ⓑ	b	ⓣ	ⓕ	t
Carol	a	b	ⓣ	t	ⓕ
Doris	ⓑ	ⓒ	ⓣ	t	ⓕ
Ellen	c	a	f	t	t

So *Doris got the most correct answers.*

Sitting Ducks

From [4], the partial seating arrangement of men and women around the table was either (M represents man and W represents woman):

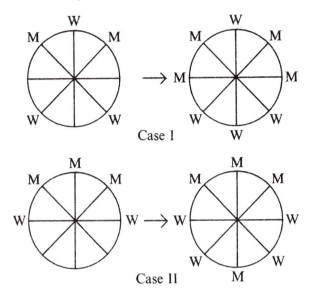

Case I

Case II

Then, from [1] and [2], either (A represents Astor, B represents Blake, and C represents Crane):

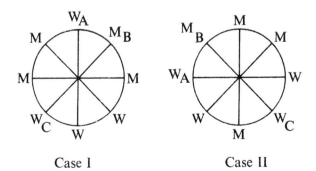

Case I   Case II

From [3], no man sat next to each one of a married couple; so, in Case I, Mrs. Blake sat opposite Mrs. Astor. But, then, no woman can sit next to each one of a married couple as required by [3]; so Case I is eliminated.

Then Case II is the correct case. Then Mrs. Blake and Mrs. Davis were seated in one of the following ways (D represents Davis):

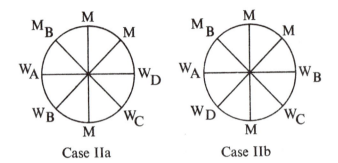

Case IIa   Case IIb

Then, in Case IIa, Mrs. Astor is the hostess who was the only person to sit next to each one of a married couple. But either Mr. Astor or Mr. Davis has to be one of the men sitting opposite each other, so that more than one person sat next to each one of a married couple. This situation contradicts [3]; so Case IIa is eliminated.

Then Case IIb is the correct case. Then Mrs. Blake or Mrs. Davis must be the hostess, from [3]. If Mrs. Blake is the hostess, then Mr. Crane sat next to her. Then Mr. Astor has to be one of the men sitting opposite each other, so that more than one person sat next to each one of a married couple. This situation contradicts [3]; so Mrs. Davis is the hostess.

Then, from [3], Mr. Astor sat next to Mrs. Davis while Mr. Davis sat next to Mrs. Blake. So Mr. Crane sat opposite Mr. Astor.

So, from [4], *Mr. Crane insulted the hostess.*

The High Suit

From [1] and [3], three different suits were led and the high suit was not led.

From [1], [2], and [3]:

(i) Clubs were not led first.

(iia) If diamonds were led first, neither clubs nor diamonds is the high suit.

(iiia) If spades were led first, neither clubs nor hearts nor spades is the high suit.

(iva) If hearts were led first, neither spades nor hearts is the high suit.

Then—from [1], [3], and [4] and from (iia), (iiia), and (iva) respectively:

(iib) If diamonds were led first, a club was led second.

(iiib) If spades were led first, a heart or a club was led second.

(ivb) If hearts were led first, a spade was led second.

The deductions above produce six possibilities as shown in the table below (C represents clubs, D represents diamonds, H represents hearts, S represents spades, and a circled letter represents the high suit):

Trick	I Suits	II Suits	III Suits	IV Suits	V Suits	VI Suits
First	D D Ⓢ	D D Ⓗ	S S Ⓓ	S S Ⓓ	H H Ⓒ	H H Ⓓ
Second	C C Ⓢ	C C Ⓗ	H H Ⓓ	C C Ⓓ	S S Ⓒ	S S Ⓓ
Third	H H Ⓢ	S S Ⓗ	C C Ⓓ	H H Ⓓ	D D Ⓒ	C C Ⓓ

Case I is eliminated because no one could have won the second trick with a spade and led a heart. Case II is eliminated because no one could have won the second trick with a heart and led a spade. Case V is eliminated because Xavier would have led the spade and both Wilson and Yoeman would have had to play a club. So, in any case, *diamonds was the high suit*.

Cases III and IV are eliminated because only Wilson could have led at the second trick after winning the first trick and only Wilson could have led at the third trick after winning the second trick, an impossible situation. Case VI is the only one possible, yielding two ways in which the fourth cards could have been played from the holdings; see below (W represents Wilson's holding, X represents Xavier's holding, etc.).

Trick	Holdings W	X	Y	Z
First	H	C	H	(D)
Second	(D)	S	H	S
Third	C	S	C	(D)

Trick	Holdings W	X	Y	Z
First	H	S	H	(D)
Second	(D)	S	C	S
Third	C	C	H	(D)

PART II
MIND PUZZLERS

Contents—Part II

Before You Begin Part II

The puzzles in Part II have a Solution Scheme for each of 34 puzzles to help the reader relate the puzzle to its solution. Two other puzzles have no Solution Scheme because of their unusual nature (see Preface); a Hint is offered instead. In addition, each puzzle after the first is given a Classification that tells the reader which of five concepts are involved in the puzzle (see Preface).

In general, a solution is reached by reasoning which eliminates the impossible situations until only the correct situation remains.

Preface

Most "logic problems" are like this one:

Pam, Ray, Sue, and Tom are an archeologist, a botanist, a chiropractor, and a dentist—though not necessarily in that order. At a party Tom said to the botanist that Sue would be along in a minute, the chiropractor congratulated the dentist on his engagement to Sue, and Pam took a picture of the chiropractor standing next to Ray. What is the occupation of each person?

With the exception of the first puzzle in Part II, which is a variation on the matching exercise above, none of the puzzles is like that one.

After the first puzzle, each Mind Puzzler involves one or more of the following:

STATEMENTS THAT MAY BE FALSE

Statements may be false because the people who make them always lie, sometimes lie, lie only at certain times, or alternately tell the truth and lie; they may be false because the people who make them are simply incorrect in what they believe to be true or in what they predict to be true; or they may be false because one of a given number of statements is said to be false, or all but one of a given number of statements are said to be false.

STATEMENTS BEGINNING WITH "IF"

A statement that contains *if* has a hypothesis and a conclusion, as in:

If I stay home tonight, then I will watch TV.

The hypothesis is: "I stay home tonight."
The conclusion is: "I will watch TV."
What is meant by saying this statement is true?
To answer this question: Suppose I don't stay home tonight. Then I am free to do whatever I want, including watching TV or not watching TV. So a false hypothesis does not make the statement false; that is, the statement is true. So

the statement is true when the hypothesis is false
and the conclusion is true

the statement is true when the hypothesis is false
and the conclusion is false

Suppose I do stay home tonight. Then, in order for the statement to be true, I must watch TV. Otherwise, the statement is false. So

the statement is true when the hypothesis is true
and the conclusion is true

the statement is false when the hypothesis is true
and the conclusion is false

A statement that contains a hypothesis and a conclusion can be called a hypothetical statement. When a hypothetical statement is true, you cannot tell whether the hypothesis is true or whether the conclusion is true. However, when a hypothetical statement is false, you know immediately that the hypothesis is true and the conclusion is false. Here is an example of a puzzle containing statements that begin with "if."

[1] If Natalie is married, then Marlene is not married.

[2] If Natalie is not married, then Loretta is married.

[3] If Marlene is married, then Loretta is not married.

Whose marital status do you know?

SOLUTION: Suppose Marlene is married. Then, from [1], Natalie is not married (otherwise, Marlene is not married) and, from [3], Loretta is not married. Then from [2], Natalie is married (otherwise, Loretta is married). Then Natalie is both married and not married. This situation is impossible. So *you know Marlene's marital status:* Marlene is not married. Then: if Natalie is not married, then Loretta is married; if Natalie is married, then you don't know whether Loretta is or not. So *you know only Marlene's marital status.*

"SUSPECTS" ASSOCIATED WITH A STRAIGHT OR A CYCLIC ORDER— A ONE-DIMENSIONAL ASSOCIATION

Straight orders include: arrival times of people at a mansion, a sequence of eliminated words paralleling a sequence of given information, ages of people, players' turns in a game, tennis-playing abilities of people, west-to-east locations of peoples' apartments, and the order in which entrants finish a race.

Cyclic orders include: a playing arrangement of people around a tennis court, a seating arrangement of people around a table, and days of the week.

A special use of ordering involves someone knowing something from the fact that someone else knows or doesn't know something. Here is an example:

[1] After being blindfolded and hatted, two men—Xavier and Yoeman—are truthfully told that either they both wear black hats or one wears a black hat and the other wears a red hat.

[2] After the blindfolds are removed, first Xavier and then Yoeman is asked to name the color of the hat on his head.

[3] The question is repeated until one man says truthfully that he does not have enough information to know the color of his hat.

Who never knows the color of his hat?

SOLUTION: Suppose Yoeman has a red hat. Then, from [1] and [2], Xavier declares he has a black hat. Then, from [1] and [2], Yoeman declares he has a red hat (because Xavier knew his color). From [3], this situation is impossible. So, from [1], Yoeman has a black hat. Then from [1] and [2], Xavier declares he doesn't know. Then, from [1] and [2], Yoeman declares he has a black hat for one of two reasons: (1) Yoeman sees a red hat on Xavier; (2) Yoeman sees a black hat on Xavier and knows that Xavier would have known the color of his hat if he had seen a red hat on Yoeman; because Xavier didn't know, Yoeman knows he has a black hat. So, because Xavier doesn't know which of the reasons Yoeman had for knowing the color of his (Yoeman's) hat, *Xavier never knows the color of his (Xavier's) hat.*

Two puzzles are of this "unusual nature," as mentioned on page 133.

"SUSPECTS" ASSOCIATED BY BLOOD TIES OR WITH VARIOUS PARTS OF A REGION— A TWO-DIMENSIONAL ASSOCIATION

Blood ties include:

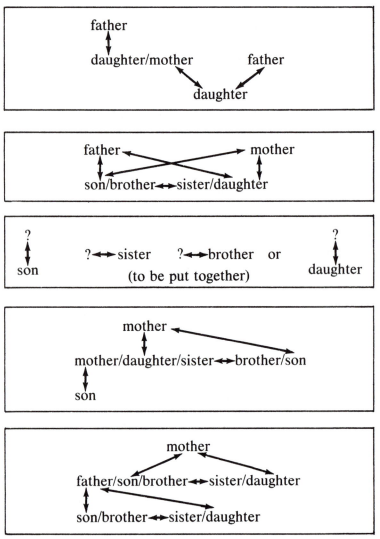

Note that each line in a chart above represents a generation, and that each person is related to the others in a chart in various ways (though relationships such as son-in-law or aunt are not shown); thus, a two-dimensional picture emerges.

Regional relationships include faces of a cube, a layout of rooms, a game board, a cross-number diagram, and a layout of cards.

A SOLUTION THAT USES COMPUTATION WITH GIVEN QUANTITIES—A MATHEMATICAL SOLUTION

Quantities include: multiples of numbers, numbers of people, digits in arithmetic, numbers in a cross-number diagram, numbers of physical traits, points scored in a game, numbers on discs, and numbers of correct predictions.

In summary, in a puzzle

(1) statements may be
(a) false
(b) hypothetical

(2) suspects may be involved in an association that is
(a) one-dimensional
(b) two-dimensional

(3) the solution may use mathematics

Each puzzle after the first is given a Classification by abbreviating the five ideas discussed above, placing the abbreviations in a chart, and inserting check marks in the appropriate columns. For example,

| Statements | | Association | | |
false	hyp.	1-dim.	2-dim.	Math.
	✔		✔	

Vera's Preference

Vera prefers her dates to be tall, dark, and handsome.

[1] Of the preferred traits—tall, dark, and handsome—no two of Adam, Boyd, Cary, and Dirk have the same number.

[2] Only Adam or Dirk is tall and fair.

[3] Only Boyd or Cary is short and handsome.

[4] Adam and Cary are either both tall or both short.

[5] Boyd and Dirk are either both dark or both fair.

Who is tall, dark, and handsome?

Solution Scheme, page 142;
Solution, page 214.

Speaking of Tennis

Four people played a tennis game.

[1] The four people were Winifred, her father, her husband, and their daughter.

After the game, one of them spoke truthfully about one time during the game:

[2] "I was directly across the net from the server's daughter.

[3] My partner (on the same side of the net as I) was directly across the net from the receiver's father.

[4] The server was diagonally across the net from the receiver (of course)."

Who spoke?

Classification and Solution Scheme, page 143; Solution, page 214.

Vera's Preference

SOLUTION SCHEME

Make a chart for yourself as follows:

	Is Adam	Is Boyd	Is Cary	Is Dirk
tall?				
dark?				
handsome?				

Write "yes" or "no" in each box so that no condition is contradicted.

Speaking of Tennis

CLASSIFICATION

Statements		Association		
false	hyp.	1-dim.	2-dim	Math.
		✔	✔	

SOLUTION SCHEME

Make a diagram for yourself as follows:

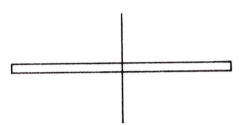

Write "Winifred," "her father," "her husband," or "their daughter" in each of the four parts of the tennis court diagram and write "server" or "receiver" in each of two parts so that no condition is contradicted.

Getting Married

Four men—Aaron, Barry, Colin, and David—and four women—Marie, Norma, Olive, and Pearl—attended a wedding.

[1] One of the four men married one of the four women.

[2] If Aaron did not get married and if Marie did not get married, then Olive got married.

[3] If Aaron did not get married and if Norma did not get married, then Barry got married.

[4] If Barry did not get married and if Olive did not get married, then Colin got married.

[5] If Colin did not get married and if Norma did not get married, then Marie got married.

Who got married?

Marie/Barry

Classification and Solution Scheme, page 146; Solution, page 215.

My House Number

My house has a number.

[1] If my house number is a multiple of 3 (0×3, 1×3, 2×3, etc.), then it is a number from 50 through 59.

[2] If my house number is not a multiple of 4, then it is a number from 60 through 69.

[3] If my house number is not a multiple of 6, then it is a number from 70 through 79.

What is my house number?

Classification and Solution Scheme, page 147. Solution, page 216.

Getting Married

Statements		Association		
false	hyp.	1-dim.	2-dim.	Math.
	✔			

SOLUTION SCHEME

Make a chart for yourself as follows:

	married Marie	married Norma	married Olive	married Pearl
Aaron				
Barry				
Colin				
David				

Place an "X" in one box so that no condition is contradicted.

My House Number

Statements		Association		
false	hyp.	1-dim.	2-dim.	Math.
	✔			✔

SOLUTION SCHEME

Make a chart for yourself as follows:

My house number is

50	51	52	53	54	55	56	57	58	59
60	61	62	63	64	65	66	67	68	69
70	71	72	73	74	75	76	77	78	79

Cross off every number that contradicts any condition.

The Murderer in the Mansion

The owner of the mansion has been murdered! The visitors to the mansion were Allen, Bixby, and Crain.

[1] The murderer, who was one of the three visitors, arrived at the mansion later than at least one of the other two visitors.

[2] A detective, who was one of the three visitors, arrived at the mansion earlier than at least one of the other two visitors.

[3] The detective arrived at the mansion at midnight.

[4] Neither Allen nor Bixby arrived at the mansion after midnight.

[5] The earlier arriver of Bixby and Crain was not the detective.

[6] The later arriver of Allen and Crain was not the murderer.

Who was the murderer?

Classification and Solution Scheme, page 150.
Solution, page 216.

Detective
Allen

The Cube

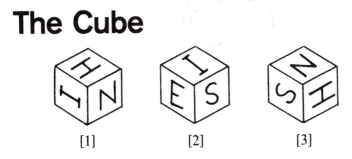

[1]　　　[2]　　　[3]

Three views of the same cube are shown above.

Which of the five letters—E, H, I, N, or S—occurs twice on the cube?

Classification and Solution Scheme, page 151.
Solution, page 217.

The Murderer in the Mansion

SOLUTION SCHEME

Make a chart for yourself as follows:

	arrived before midnight	arrived at midnight	arrived after midnight
Allen			
Bixby			
Crain			
The murderer			
The detective			

Place an "X" in each of five boxes so that no condition is contradicted.

The Cube

CLASSIFICATION

Statements		Association		
false	hyp.	1-dim.	2-dim.	Math.
			✔	

SOLUTION SCHEME

Draw a multiview cube as shown below:

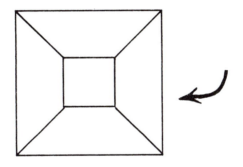

Place "E," "H," "I," "N," or "S" on each face of this multiview cube and at the arrow (to indicate the only face not seen) so that no condition is contradicted.

Three-Letter Word

Here is a list of words:

INN   PEN   PET   PIE   TEE   TIE

[1] Three logicians are told, "I have told each of you one of the three letters in a word listed before you so that the three known letters together spell the word."

[2] Then they are told, "None of you can tell how many vowels the word has."

[3] Then they are told, "At this point still none of you can tell how many vowels the word has."

[4] Then one of the three logicians says he knows what the word is.

What is the word?

Classification and Solution Scheme, page 154; Solution, page 218.

Esther's Fiancé

Esther is engaged.

[1] Her fiancé is either Arthur, Barton, Claude, or Dexter.

[2] Each of the four men and Esther either always tells the truth or always lies.

[3] Arthur says: "Exactly one of us four men always tells the truth."

[4] Barton says: "Exactly one of us four men always lies."

[5] Claude says: "Arthur or Barton is Esther's fiancé."

[6] Esther says: "My fiancé and I either both always tell the truth or both always lie."

Who is Esther's fiancé?

Classification and Solution
Scheme, page 155;
Solution, page 218.

Three-Letter Word

CLASSIFICATION

Statements		Association		
false	hyp.	1-dim.	2-dim.	Math.
		✔		

SOLUTION SCHEME

Make a chart for yourself as follows:

After the declaration was made in	none of the three logicians could have been told the word had a(n)				
	E	I	N	P	T
[2]					
[3]					

Place an "X" in one box of each row so that no condition is contradicted.

Esther's Fiancé

CLASSIFICATION

Statements		Association		
false	hyp.	1-dim.	2-dim.	Math.
✔				

SOLUTION SCHEME

Make a chart for yourself as follows:

	always tells the truth	always lies
Arthur		
Barton		
Claude		
Dexter		
Esther's fiancé		

Place an "X" in one box in each row so that no condition is contradicted.

Family Occupations

One of four people is a singer and another is a dancer.

[1] The four people are Mr. Brown, his wife, their son, and their daughter.

[2] If the singer and the dancer are the same sex, then the dancer is older than the singer.

[3] If neither the singer nor the dancer is the parent of the other, then the singer is older than the dancer.

[4] If the singer is a man, then the singer and the dancer are the same age.

[5] If the singer and the dancer are of opposite sex, then the man is older than the woman.

Whose occupation do you know?

Classification and Solution Scheme, page 158; Solution, page 219.

A Small Party

"At the party: I ♥ Kyra

[1] There were 9 men and children.

[2] There were 2 more women than children.

[3] The number of different man-woman couples possible was 24. (If there were 10 men and 5 women at the party, then there would have been 10 × 5 or 50 man-woman couples possible.)

Of the three groups—men, women, and children—at the party:

[4] There were 4 of one group.

[5] There were 6 of one group.

[6] There were 8 of one group."

[7] Exactly one of the speaker's statements is false.

Which of [1] through [6] is false?

Classification and Solution Scheme, page 159; Solution, page 219.

Family Occupations

CLASSIFICATION

Statements		Association		
false	hyp.	1-dim.	2-dim.	Math.
	✔	✔	✔	

SOLUTION SCHEME

Make a chart for yourself as follows:

Singer	Dancer

Write "Mr. Brown," "his wife," "their son," or "their daughter" in each box in as many ways as possible—crossing off any unused boxes—so that no condition is contradicted.

A Small Party

Statements		Association		
false	hyp.	1-dim.	2-dim.	Math.
✔				✔

SOLUTION SCHEME

Make a chart for yourself as follows:

	men	women	children
Number of			

Write a number in each box so that no condition is contradicted.

The Separated Couple

Mr. and Mrs. Alden, Mr. and Mrs. Brent, Mr. and Mrs. Crown, and Mr. and Mrs. Drake were seated around a table.

[1] Their chairs were arranged around the square table like this:

[2] The person sitting across from Mrs. Alden was a man who sat on Mr. Brent's immediate left.

[3] The person sitting on Mrs. Crown's immediate left was a man who sat across from Mr. Drake.

[4] Only one couple did not sit next to each other and this couple did not sit across from each other.

Which couple did not sit next to each other?

Classification and Solution Scheme, page 162; Solution, page 220.

The Opposite Sex

Carmen, Evelyn, Leslie, and Marion are related.

[1] Carmen or Evelyn is Leslie's only son.

[2] Evelyn or Leslie is Marion's sister.

[3] Marion is Carmen's brother or only daughter.

[4] One of the four is the opposite sex from each of the other three.

Who is the opposite sex from each of the others?

Classification and Solution Scheme, page 163; Solution, page 221.

L M
C(m)

Evelyn

The Separated Couple

Statements		Association		
false	hyp.	1-dim.	2-dim.	Math.
		✔		

SOLUTION SCHEME

Make a diagram for yourself as follows:

Using the symbols M_A for Alden man, W_A for Alden woman, etc., place the Aldens, Brents, Crowns, and Drakes around the table so that no condition is contradicted.

The Opposite Sex

CLASSIFICATION

Statements		Association		
false	hyp.	1-dim.	2-dim.	Math.
			✔	

SOLUTION SCHEME

Make a chart for yourself as follows:

	Leslie's only son	Marion's sister	Carmen's brother	Carmen's only daughter
Carmen is			▨	▨
Evelyn is				
Leslie is	▨			
Marion is		▨		

Place an "X" in each of three boxes so that no condition is contradicted.

Truth Day

Philip lies a lot.

[1] He tells the truth on only one of the days of the week.

[2] The days of the week in order are: Sunday, Monday, Tuesday, Wednesday, Thursday, Friday, Saturday, Sunday, Monday, etc.

[3] One day he said: "I lie on Mondays and Tuesdays."

[4] The next day he said: "Today is either Thursday, Saturday, or Sunday."

[5] The next day he said: "I lie on Wednesdays and Fridays."

On which day of the week does Philip tell the truth?

Classification and Solution
Scheme, page 166;
Solution, page 221.

The Murderer in the Hotel

Arlene, Brenda, Cheryl, Daniel, Emmett, and Farley stayed in a hotel.

[1] Each stayed in a different one of six rooms as shown here:

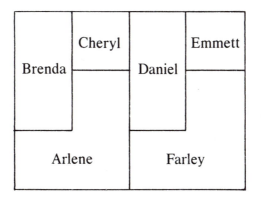

[2] One of the six murdered one of the other five.

[3] If the murderer and the victim stayed in rooms that did not border on each other, then Arlene or Farley was the victim.

[4] If the murderer and the victim stayed in rooms that bordered on different numbers of rooms, then Brenda or Cheryl was the murderer.

[5] If the murderer and the victim stayed in rooms that were different in size, then Daniel or Emmett was the murderer.

Who was the murderer?

Classification and Solution
Scheme, page 167;
Solution, page 222.

Truth Day

Statements		Association		
false	hyp.	1-dim.	2-dim.	Math.
✔		✔		

SOLUTION SCHEME

Make a chart for yourself as follows:

	Sun	Mon	Tues	Wed	Thurs	Fri	Sat
Declaration in [3] was made on a:							
Declaration in [4] was made on a:							
Declaration in [5] was made on a:							

Place an "X" in one box in each row so that no condition is contradicted.

The Murderer in the Hotel

CLASSIFICATION

Statements		Association		
false	hyp.	1-dim.	2-dim.	Math.
	✔		✔	

SOLUTION SCHEME

Make a chart for yourself as follows:

	is the murderer	is the victim
Arlene		
Brenda		
Cheryl		
Daniel		
Emmett		
Farley		

Place an "X" in one box in each column so that no condition is contradicted.

The Three Groups

Anita, Beryl, and Chloe live on an island inhabited by three groups: the Trusties, the Fibbers, and the Normals.

[1] Each is either a Trusty who always tells the truth, a Fibber who always lies, or a Normal who may do either.

[2] Anita says: "If we are all from the same group, then that group is the Fibbers."

[3] Beryl says: "If just one of us belongs to a different group from each of the others, then that one is a Fibber."

[4] Chloe says: "If each of us belongs to a different group from each of the others, then I am a Fibber."

Whose group do you know?

Classification and Solution
Scheme, page 170;
Solution, page 223.

Code Word

$$S \quad L \quad I \quad D \quad E$$
$$- \quad D \quad E \quad A \quad N$$
$$\overline{\quad 3 \quad 6 \quad 5 \quad 1}$$

Each of seven digits from 0, 1, 2, 3, 4, 5, 6, 7, 8, and 9 is represented by a different letter in the subtraction problem above.

What word represents 3 6 5 1?

Classification and Solution
Scheme, page 171;
Solution, page 224.

The Three Groups

CLASSIFICATION

Statements		Association		
false	hyp.	1-dim.	2-dim.	Math.
✔	✔			

SOLUTION SCHEME

Make a chart for yourself as follows:

Anita	Beryl	Chloe

Write "Trusty," "Fibber," or "Normal" in each box in as many ways as possible—crossing off any unused boxes—so that no condition is contradicted.

Code Word

Statements		Association		
false	hyp.	1-dim.	2-dim.	Math.
				✔

SOLUTION SCHEME

Make a chart for yourself as follows:

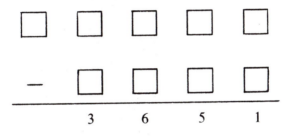

Write a digit in each box—to discover its corresponding letter—so that the one condition is not contradicted.

The Winning Mark

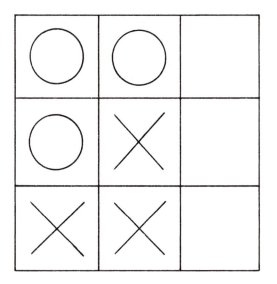

The game of tic-tac-toe is played in a large square divided into nine small squares.

[1] Each of two players in turn places his or her mark—usually X or O—in a small square.

[2] The player who first gets three marks in a horizontal, vertical, or diagonal line wins.

[3] A player will always place his or her mark in a line that already contains (a) two of his or her own marks or (b) two of his or her opponent's marks—giving (a) priority over (b).

Only the last mark to be placed in the game shown above is not given.

Which mark—X or O—wins the game?

Classification and Solution Scheme, page 174; Solution, page 225.

A Big Party

Someone is heard to say truthfully:

[1] "At the party there were
   14 adults,
   17 children,
   12 males, and
   19 females.

[2] Then I arrived and the number of different man-woman couples possible became equal to the number of different boy-girl couples possible. (If there were 6 men and 8 women at the party, then there would have been 6 × 8 or 48 man-woman couples possible.)"

Is the speaker a man, a woman, a boy, or a girl?

Classification and Solution Scheme, page 175; Solution, page 226.

The Winning Mark

SOLUTION SCHEME

Make a diagram for yourself as follows:

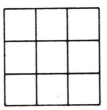

Write "fifth" or "sixth" in each of two small squares in the diagram (to indicate the order in which the marks were placed in the diagram) so that no condition is contradicted.

A Big Party

Statements		Association		
false	hyp.	1-dim.	2-dim.	Math.
				✔

SOLUTION SCHEME

Make a chart for yourself as follows:

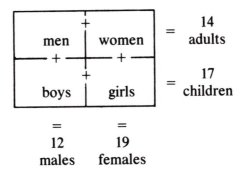

Write a number in each box so that [2] is not contra-dicted.

The Tennis Game

Four people are about to play a tennis game.

[1] The four people are Mr. and Mrs. Jones and Mr. and Mrs. Smith.

[2] The worst player is directly across the net from the better Jones player.

[3] The better male player is diagonally across the net from the poorer Smith player.

[4] The poorer male and the better female players are on the same side of the net.

Who is the best player?

Classification and Solution Scheme, page 178; Solution, page 229.

Multiples of 7

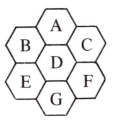

When completed, this cross-number puzzle has:

[1] Exactly one digit—0, 1, 2, 3, 4, 5, 6, 7, 8, or 9—in each hexagonal box.

[2] Only numbers that are multiples of seven (0×7, 1×7, 2×7, etc.) when read down and diagonally downward toward the right and left (BE, ADG, CF; AC, BDF, EG; AB, CDE, FG).

[3] No two numbers the same.

What number does ADG represent?

Classification and Solution Scheme, page 179; Solution, page 230.

The Tennis Game

CLASSIFICATION

Statements		Association		
false	hyp.	1-dim.	2-dim.	Math.
		✔✔		

SOLUTION SCHEME

Make a diagram for yourself as follows:

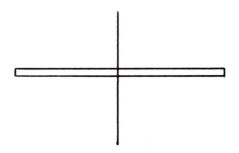

Write "Mr. Jones," "Mrs. Jones," "Mr. Smith," or "Mrs. Smith" in each of the four parts of the tennis-court diagram and write "worst," "better Jones," "better male," "poorer Smith," "poorer male," or "better female" in each of the four parts so that no condition is contradicted.

Multiples of 7

CLASSIFICATION

Statements		Association		
false	hyp.	1-dim.	2-dim.	Math.
			✔	✔

SOLUTION SCHEME

Make a diagram for yourself as follows:

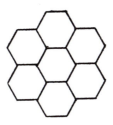

Write a digit (0, 1, 2, 3, 4, 5, 6, 7, 8, 9) in each box so that no one condition is contradicted.

Harry Will Marry

Harry will marry April, Bette, or Clare.

[1] Of April and Bette:
   (a) Either both have hazel eyes or both do not.
   (b) One is red-haired and the other is not.

[2] Of April and Clare:
   (a) Either both are red-haired or both are not.
   (b) One is slender and the other is not.

[3] Of Bette and Clare:
   (a) One has hazel eyes and the other does not.
   (b) One is slender and the other is not.

[4] Of the mentioned characteristics—hazel eyes, red-haired, and slender:
   (a) If any of April, Bette, and Clare has exactly two of these characteristics, then Harry will marry only the woman with the least number of them.
   (b) If any of April, Bette, and Clare has exactly one of these characteristics, then Harry will marry only the woman with the greatest number of them.

Who will Harry marry?

Classification and Solution Scheme, page 182; Solution, page 232.

The President

Aubrey, Blaine, and Curtis live on an island inhabited by three groups: the Truthtellers, the Falsifiers, and the Alternators.

[1] Each is either a Truthteller who always tells the truth, a Falsifier who always lies, or an Alternator who alternately tells the truth and lies.

[2] One of the three is President of the island.

[3] Aubrey says: (a) "The President belongs to a different group from each of the other two of us."
(b) "Blaine is not the President."

[4] Blaine says: (a) "The President is a Falsifier."
(b) "Aubrey is not the President."

[5] Curtis says: (a) "Exactly two of us belong to the same group."
(b) "I am not the President."

Who is the President?

*Classification and Solution
Scheme, page 183;
Solution, page 233.*

Harry Will Marry

CLASSIFICATION

Statements		Association		
false	hyp.	1-dim.	2-dim.	Math.
	✔			

SOLUTION SCHEME

Make a chart for yourself as follows:

	Is April	Is Bette	Is Clare
hazel-eyed?			
red-haired?			
slender?			

Write "yes" or "no" in each box so that no condition is contradicted.

The President

Statements		Association		
false	hyp.	1-dim.	2-dim.	Math.
✔				

SOLUTION SCHEME

Make a chart for yourself as follows:

	is true	is false
[3a]		
[3b]		
[4a]		
[4b]		
[5a]		
[5b]		

Place an "X" in one box in each row so that no condition is contradicted.

Apartments

Avery, Blake, Clark, and Doyle each live in an apartment.

[1] Their apartments are arranged like this:

a	b	c	d

→ East

[2] One of the four is the landlord.

[3] If Clark's apartment is not next to Blake's apartment, then the landlord is Avery and lives in apartment a.

[4] If Avery's apartment is east of Clark's apartment, then the landlord is Doyle and lives in apartment d.

[5] If Blake's apartment is not next to Doyle's apartment, then the landlord is Clark and lives in apartment c.

[6] If Doyle's apartment is east of Avery's apartment, then the landlord is Blake and lives in apartment b.

Who is the landlord?

Classification and Solution Scheme, page 186; Solution, page 234.

Murderer's Occupation

In attempting to solve a murder, six detectives each arrived at a different one of the following descriptions of the murderer.

	Occupation	Sex	Height in inches	Weight in pounds	Age in years	Smoker
[1]	author	male	63 to 66	110 to 130	20 to 30	cigarette
[2]	barber	female	66 to 69	130 to 150	30 to 40	cigar
[3]	cooper	male	69 to 72	130 to 150	20 to 30	pipe
[4]	draper	male	63 to 66	150 to 170	40 to 50	cigar
[5]	editor	female	63 to 66	170 to 190	20 to 30	cigarette
[6]	farmer	female	72 to 75	110 to 130	50 to 60	non-

It turned out that:

[7] Each detective was correct in the same number of the six listed particulars as any other detective.

[8] Exactly one of each kind of particular was correct.

What was the occupation of the murderer?

Classification and Solution Scheme, page 187; Solution, page 235.

Apartments

CLASSIFICATION

Statements		Association		
false	hyp.	1-dim.	2-dim.	Math.
	✔	✔		

SOLUTION SCHEME

Make a diagram for yourself as follows:

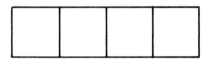

Write "Avery," "Blake," "Clark," or "Doyle" in each box so that no condition is contradicted.

Murderer's Occupation

CLASSIFICATION

Statements		Association		
false	hyp.	1-dim.	2-dim.	Math.
✔				✔

SOLUTION SCHEME

Make a chart for yourself as follows:

Occupation	Sex	Height in inches	Weight in pounds	Age in years	Smoker
author	male	63 to 66	110 to 130	20 to 30	cigarette
barber	female	66 to 69	130 to 150	30 to 40	cigar
cooper	male	69 to 72	130 to 150	20 to 30	pipe
draper	male	63 to 66	150 to 170	40 to 50	cigar
editor	female	63 to 66	170 to 190	20 to 30	cigarette
farmer	female	72 to 75	110 to 130	50 to 60	non-

Cross off entries in the boxes (to indicate incorrect information) so that neither [7] nor [8] is contradicted.

The Owner of the Table

Six people were seated around a table.

[1] Their chairs were arranged around the rectangular table like this:

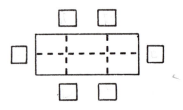

[2] The six people were three women—Althea, Blythe, and Cecile—and three men—Dudley, Edward, and Foster.

[3] Althea sat opposite Blythe or Dudley.

[4] Edward sat to the immediate left of Cecile.

[5] Foster sat to the immediate left of one woman and to the immediate right of another woman.

[6] The person who owned the table was the only person who sat both opposite a man and to the immediate left of a woman.

Who owned the table?

Classification and Solution Scheme, page 190; Solution, page 237.

Family Murder

Statement I. I am the mother of the murderer, but not the mother of the victim.

Statement II. I am the mother of the victim, but not the mother of the murderer.

Statement III. I am the same sex as the victim.

Of the statements above and the people who made them:

[1] Each statement was made by a different one of four people—Alice, her mother, her brother (her mother's son), and her son.

[2] The one person of these four who made no statement is the victim, murdered by one of the other three.

[3] Exactly one of the three statements is false.

Who is the murderer?

Classification and Solution Scheme, page 191; Solution, page 238.

The Owner of the Table

CLASSIFICATION

Statements		Association		
false	hyp.	1-dim.	2-dim.	Math.
		✔		

SOLUTION SCHEME

Make a diagram for yourself as follows:

Using the symbols A for Althea, B for Blythe, C for Cecile, D for Dudley, E for Edward, and F for Foster, place the people around the table so that no condition is contradicted.

Family Murder

CLASSIFICATION

Statements		Association		
false	hyp.	1-dim.	2-dim.	Math.
✔			✔	

SOLUTION SCHEME

Make a chart for yourself as follows:

	made Statement I	made Statement II	made Statement III	made the false statement
Alice				
Her mother				
Her brother				
Her son				
The murderer				

Place an "X" in each of five boxes so that no condition is contradicted.

The Dart Game

Three men—Arnold, Buford, and Conrad—played a dart game.

[1] Each dart that lodged in the game board scored 1, 5, 10, 25, 50, or 100 points.

[2] Each man threw nine darts that lodged in the board.

[3] Each man's total score was the same as any other man's total score.

[4] No number of points scored by a dart was scored by more than one man.

[5] Arnold scored all the 5s and Buford scored all the 10s.

Who scored all the 100s?

Classification and Solution Scheme, page 194; Solution, page 240.

Hotel Rooms

Six people stayed at a hotel.

[1] The six people were three men—Arden, Brian, and Clyde—and three women.

[2] Each stayed in a different one of six rooms arranged like this:

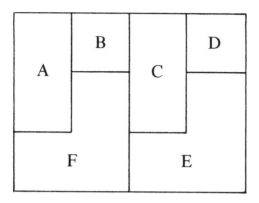

[3] Arden said: "I stayed in a large room."

[4] Brian said: "I stayed in a medium-sized room."

[5] Clyde said: "I stayed in a small room."

[6] Exactly one man lied.

[7] Of the three rooms occupied by the men, only the room occupied by the man who lied bordered on exactly two of the rooms occupied by the women.

Who lied?

Classification and Solution Scheme, page 195; Solution, page 241.

The Dart Game

Statements		Association		
false	hyp.	1-dim.	2-dim.	Math.
				✔

SOLUTION SCHEME

Make a chart for yourself as follows:

	1s	5s	10s	25s	50s	100s	scored this total number of points
		scored this number of					
Arnold							
Buford							
Conrad							

Write a number in each box so that no condition is contradicted.

Hotel Rooms

SOLUTION SCHEME

Make a diagram for yourself as follows:

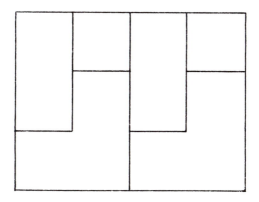

Write "Arden," "Brian," or "Clyde" in each of three parts of the diagram and write "woman" in each of the remaining three parts so that no condition is contradicted.

The Numbered Discs

Three women were seated around a table.

[1] After the three women were blindfolded, a numbered disc was pasted on each of their foreheads.

[2] The women were then truthfully told "Each of you has either a 1, a 2, or a 3 on your forehead, and the sum of your numbers is either 6 or 7."

[3] After the blindfolds were removed, each woman in turn was asked to name the number on her forehead without seeing it.

[4] The question was repeated until only one woman failed to name the number on her forehead.

[5] When it was logically possible to name the number on her forehead, each woman did so; when it was not logically possible to name the number on her forehead, each woman said "I do not know the number" and waited until the question was repeated to her next time around.

[6] Each of the three women had a 2 on her forehead.

Which woman failed to name her number: the first woman asked, the second woman asked, or the third woman asked?

Classification and Hint,
page 198;
Solution, page 242.

Finishing First

Here are various predictions on the order in which some entrants in a race would finish, together with a summary of how correct each prediction was.

	first	second	third	fourth	fifth	Number of entrants finishing in first through fifth positions that were predicted in the	
	Predictions on the entrant finishing					right position	wrong position
[1]	Ada	Bea	Cal	Don	Eve	2	1
[2]	Flo	Guy	Hal	Eve	Don	0	1
[3]	Guy	Cal	Eve	Ida	Jan	0	2
[4]	Flo	Guy	Ken	Bea	Ida	1	2
[5]	Guy	Flo	Eve	Ada	Cal	1	1

Who finished first in the race?

Classification and Solution
Scheme, page 199;
Solution, page 244.

The Numbered Discs

HINT

Assume the women are questioned in a clockwise order. Then the woman at the →, who is the woman clockwise to the woman at the ?, knows the woman at the ? sees either:

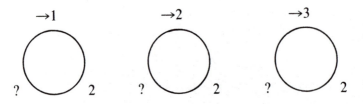

Finishing First

CLASSIFICATION

Statements		Association		
false	hyp.	1-dim.	2-dim.	Math.
✔		✔		✔

SOLUTION SCHEME

Make a chart for yourself as follows:

First	Second	Third	Fourth	Fifth

Write "Ada," "Bea," "Cal," "Don," "Eve," "Flo," "Guy," "Hal," "Ida," "Jan," or "Ken" in each box so that no condition is contradicted.

The Lead in the Play

Five adults were in a play.

[1] The five adults were Tyrone, his sister, their mother, his son, and his daughter.

[2] Each adult had a different one of five dressing rooms arranged like this:

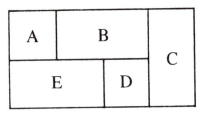

[3] The dressing room of the lead in the play and the dressing room of the lead's sibling bordered on the same number of rooms.

[4] The dressing room of the lead and the dressing room of the lead's parent were the same size.

[5] Tyrone's dressing room did not border on his daughter's dressing room.

[6] Everyone's dressing room bordered on at least one other man-occupied room and one other woman-occupied room.

Who was the lead?

*Classification and Solution
Scheme, page 202.
Solution, page 245.*

The Center Card

There are nine cards.

[1] The cards are arranged like this:

[2] Every ace borders on a king and on a queen.

[3] Every king borders on a queen and on a jack.

[4] Every queen borders on a jack.

[5] There are at least two aces, two kings, two queens, and two jacks.

What kind of card is in the center?

*Classification and Solution
Scheme, page 203;
Solution, page 246.*

The Lead in the Play

CLASSIFICATION

Statements		Association		
false	hyp.	1-dim.	2-dim.	Math.
			✔✔	

SOLUTION SCHEME

Make a diagram for yourself as follows:

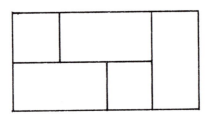

Write "Tyrone," "his sister," "their mother," "his son," or "his daughter" in each of the five parts of the diagram so that no condition is contradicted.

The Center Card

Statements		Association		
false	hyp.	1-dim.	2-dim.	Math.
			✔	

SOLUTION SCHEME

Make a diagram for yourself as follows:

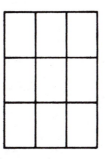

Write "ace," "king," "queen," or "jack" in each part of the diagram so that no condition is contradicted.

Dogs and Cats

Angus, Basil, Craig, and Duane have pets.

[1] Angus says: "If Duane and I each have a dog, then exactly one of Basil and Craig has a dog."

[2] Basil says: "If Craig and I each have a cat, then exactly one of Angus and Duane has a dog."

[3] Craig says: "If Angus and I each have a dog, then exactly one of Basil and Duane has a cat."

[4] Duane says: "If Basil and I each have a cat, then exactly one of Basil and I has a dog."

[5] Only one of the four is telling the truth.

Who is telling the truth?

Classification and Solution Scheme, page 206; Solution, page 248.

A—
B—
C—
D—

The Omitted Age

When completed, this cross-number puzzle

[1] Has exactly one digit—0, 1, 2, 3, 4, 5, 6, 7, 8, or 9—in each box.

[2] Has no zero in a box that contains a, b, c, or d.

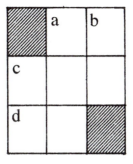

[3] Has these definitions:

ACROSS

a. Abigail's age

c. Sum of Abigail's age, Blanche's age, Cynthia's age, and Darlene's age

d. Blanche's age

DOWN

a. Sum of three of the ages in c across

b. Cynthia's age

c. Darlene's age

Whose age was omitted from a down?

Classification and Solution Scheme, page 207; Solution, page 249.

Dogs and Cats

Statements		Association		
false	hyp.	1-dim.	2-dim.	Math.
✔	✔			

SOLUTION SCHEME

Make a chart for yourself as follows:

	Does Angus	Does Basil	Does Craig	Does Duane
have a dog?				
have a cat?				

Write "yes" or "no" in each box so that no condition is contradicted.

The Omitted Age

CLASSIFICATION

Statements		Association		
false	hyp.	1-dim.	2-dim.	Math.
			✔	✔

SOLUTION SCHEME

Make a diagram and charts for yourself as follows:

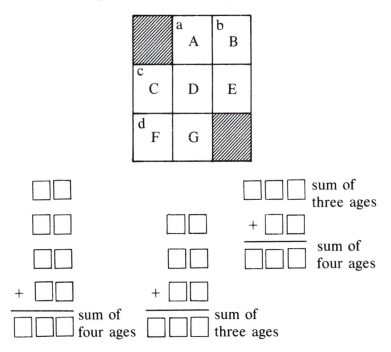

Write "A," "B," "C," "D," "E," "F," or "G" in each box of the charts so that no condition is contradicted and so that no addition is impossible.

The Hats

Four men were seated around a table.

[1] After the four men were blindfolded, a colored hat was placed on each of their heads.

[2] The men were then truthfully told: "The hat on each of your heads was chosen from among two white hats, two black hats, and one red hat."

[3] After the fifth hat was taken away, the blindfolds were removed and each man in turn was asked to name the color of the hat on his head without seeing it.

[4] The question was repeated until only one man failed to name the color of the hat on his head.

[5] When it was logically possible to name the color of the hat on his head, each man did so; when it was not logically possible to name the color of the hat on his head, each man said "I do not know the color" and waited until the question was repeated to him the next time around.

[6] None of the four men received the red hat.

Which man failed to name the color of his hat: the first man asked, the second man asked, the third man asked, or the fourth man asked?

Classification and Hint,
page 211;
Solution, page 251.

The Dart Board

Three women—Alma, Bess, and Cleo—played a dart game.

[1] Here is the dart board they used:

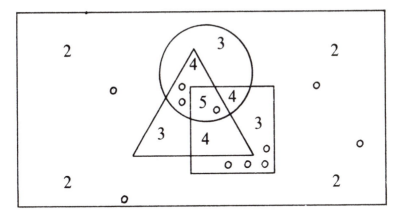

[a] Where a player's dart lodged in the board is indicated by o.

[b] The number of points scored by a dart, when it lodged in one of the various regions on the board, is indicated by 2, 3, 4, or 5.

[2] Each woman's total score was the same as any other woman's total score.

[3] Alma said: "If I was the first to score in the square, then I scored at least one 2."

[4] Bess said: "If I was the first to score in the triangle, then Alma and Cleo did not score the same number of 2s."

[5] Cleo said: "If I was the first to score in the circle, then I did not score more 2s than Bess."

[6] Only one woman told the truth.

Who scored the 5?

Classification and Solution Scheme, page 212; Solution, page 254.

The Hats

HINT

Let X represent one color hat of two black hats and two white hats, and let Y represent the other color hat; let R represent a red hat. Assume the men are questioned in a clockwise order. Then the man at the →, who is the man clockwise to the man at the ?, knows the man at the ? sees either:

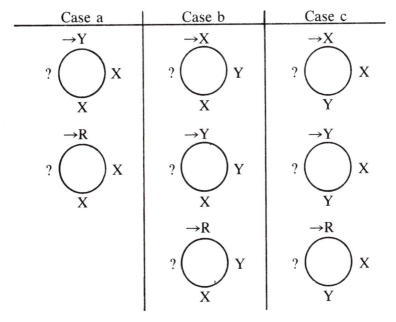

| Case a | Case b | Case c |

211

The Dart Board

CLASSIFICATION

Statements		Association		
false	hyp.	1-dim.	2-dim.	Math.
✔	✔	✔	✔	✔

SOLUTION SCHEME

Make a chart for yourself as follows:

	scored this number of				scored this total number of points
	2s	3s	4s	5s	
Alma					
Bess					
Cleo					

Write a number in each box so that no condition is contradicted.

Solutions

Vera's Preference

From [1]: (I) exactly one of Adam, Boyd, Cary, and Dirk has none of the preferred traits; (II) exactly one of Adam, Boyd, Cary, and Dirk has all of the preferred traits.

So, from [4] and [5]: either (x) Adam and Cary are both tall and Boyd and Dirk are both fair; or (y) Adam and Cary are both short and Boyd and Dirk are both dark. From [2], y is impossible; so x is the correct situation.

Then, from [3], Boyd is short and handsome. Then, from I, Dirk is short and unhandsome. Then, from [2]), Adam is fair. Then, from II, Cary is dark and handsome. So, *Cary is tall, dark, and handsome.*

Then, from [1], Adam is handsome.

Speaking of Tennis

From [2] and [3]:

speaker	speaker's partner
server's daughter	receiver's father

Then, from [4], either:

speaker	speaker's partner server
server's daughter receiver	receiver's father

Case I

speaker receiver	speaker's partner
server's daughter	receiver's father server

Case II

Then, in Case II, the receiver's father/server was the father of both the receiver and the server's daughter. From [1], this situation is impossible. So Case II is not a correct case.

Then Case I is a correct case. Then the server's daughter/receiver was the daughter of both the server and the receiver's father. So, from [1], the server's daughter/receiver was Winifred's daughter, the receiver's father was Winifred's husband, and the server was Winifred. Then, from [1], Winifred's father was the fourth player, the speaker. So *Winifred's father spoke.*

Note: If the speaker is placed in the upper right instead of the upper left of the diagram, then the placement of the players will be

speaker's partner server	speaker
receiver's father	server's daughter receiver

but the corresponding identities of the players remain the same.

Getting Married

Suppose Aaron got married. Then, from [1] and [4], Aaron married Olive. But this situation is impossible, from [1] and [5].

Suppose Colin got married. Then, from [1] and [3], Colin married Norma. But this situation is impossible, from [1] and [2].

Suppose David got married. Then, from [3] and [4], David married Norma and Olive. But this situation is impossible, from [1].

So, from [1], Barry got married.

From [1] and [2], Barry did not marry Norma. From [1] and [5], Barry did not marry Olive. From [1] and [2] or from [1] and [5], Barry did not marry Pearl.

So, from [1], *Barry and Marie got married.*

My House Number

Suppose my house number is a multiple of 3. Then, from [1], it is either 51, 54, or 57. But, from [2], it cannot be any of these numbers because none is a multiple of 4. So my house number is not a multiple of 3.

Then my house number is not a multiple of 6 because a multiple of 6 is a multiple of 3. So, from [3], it is a number from 70 through 79. Then, because it is not a multiple of 3, it is either 70, 71, 73, 74, 76, 77, or 79.

Then, from [2], it cannot be "not a multiple of 4," so it *is* a multiple of 4. Then *my house number is 76*, because it is either 70, 71, 73, 74, 76, 77, or 79, and of these only 76 is a multiple of 4.

The Murderer in the Mansion

From [2] and [3], the detective arrived at midnight and at least one of the three visitors arrived after midnight. Then, from [4], Crain arrived after midnight. So Crain was not the detective. Then, from [4] and [5], Bixby was not the detective. So, from [2], Allen was the detective. Then, from [6],

Crain was not the murderer. Then, from [1] and [4], Allen arrived after Bixby and *Allen was the murderer*.

In summary: Bixby arrived before midnight; Allen, who was both detective and murderer, arrived at midnight; and Crain arrived after midnight.

The Cube

Either S occurs twice or S occurs once on the cube.

If S occurs twice on the cube: then, from [2],

Then, from [1], 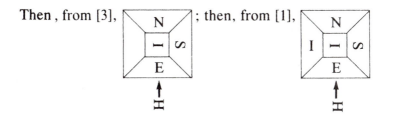 and H would have to be on the

face where E is. This situation is impossible.

So S occurs once on the cube. Then, from [2],

Then, from [3], ; then, from [1],

So *I occurs twice on the cube.*

Three-Letter Word

From [1] and [2], none of the three logicians was told the word had an N; otherwise a logician would know that the word had one vowel. So the word is not INN or PEN.

Then, from [1] and [3], none of the three logicians was told the word had an I; otherwise a logician would know the word, now one of four, had two vowels. So the word is not PIE or TIE.

Then, from [1] and [4], the logician who knows the word must have been told a letter that is in only one of the two remaining words, PET and TEE. So that logician was told the word had a P and *the word is PET*.

Esther's Fiancé

From [2] and [6]: If Esther always tells the truth, then her fiancé always tells the truth; if Esther always lies, then her fiancé always tells the truth. So Esther's fiancé always tells the truth.

Then, from [1] and [2]: If the declaration in [5] is false, then Claude lied and Dexter is the truth-telling fiancé. Then the declaration in [3] is false. Then the declaration in [4] is false. Then the declaration in [3] is true. Because the declaration in [3] is both false and true, this situation is impossible. So the declaration in [5] is true.

Then, from a true declaration in [5], the declaration in [3] is false. Then, because Esther's fiancé always tells the truth, *Barton is Esther's fiancé*. Then the declaration in [4] is true. Then Dexter always tells the truth.

Esther's declaration in [6] may be either true or false.

Family Occupations

From [2] and [4], the singer and the dancer are not both men. From [4] and [5], if the singer is a man, then the dancer must be a man. So the singer is a woman and either:

	Singer is a	Dancer is a
Case I	woman	woman
Case II	woman	man

Suppose Case I is true. Then, from [1] and [2], the dancer is Mr. Brown's wife and the singer is Mr. Brown's daughter.

Suppose Case II is true. Then, from [1], [3], and [5], the singer and the dancer are neither Mr. Brown's wife and Mr. Brown, respectively, nor Mr. Brown's daughter and Mr. Brown's son, respectively. Then, from [1] and [5], the dancer is Mr. Brown and the singer is Mr. Brown's daughter.

So, in either case, you know *Mr. Brown's daughter is the singer.*

A Small Party

Suppose [4] through [6] are all true. Then [1] is false, and [2] and [3] cannot both be true. From [7], this situation is impossible.

So, from [7], one of [4] through [6] is false, and [1] through [3] are all true. Then, from [1] and [2], there were 11 men and women. Then, from [3], either: (A) there were 8 men and 3 women; or (B) there were 3 men and 8 women.

Suppose A is correct. Then, from [2], there was 1 child. Then [4] and [5] are both false, contradicting [7]. So A is not correct.

Then B is correct. Then, from [2], there were 6 children. Then *[4] is false*.

The Separated Couple

From [1] and [2], either (W_A is Alden woman, M is man, and M_B is Brent man):

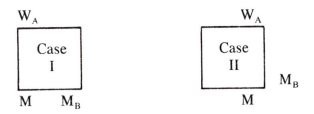

Then the man sitting across from Mrs. Alden was not Mr. Drake, from [3], and was not Mr. Alden, from [4]. So the man sitting across from Mrs. Alden was Mr. Crown.

Then, from [3], the man who sat on Mrs. Crown's immediate left was Mr. Alden and, from [3], Mrs. Crown could not have sat in chair h in Case I, nor in chair a or f in Case II. From [4], Mrs. Crown could not have sat in chair b, c, or d in Case I, nor in chair c or g in Case II. So Mrs. Crown sat either in chair g in Case I or in chair h in Case II. So, from [3] and [4], either (W_C is Crown woman, M_A is Alden man, M_C is Crown man, and M_D is Drake man):

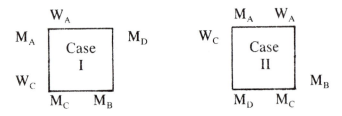

Then, from [4], Case I is impossible because either the Blakes sat next to each other and the Drakes sat next to each other, or the Blakes sat across from each other. So Case II is the correct one. Then *the Crowns did not sit next to each other* and, from [4], Mrs. Brent and Mrs. Drake each sat next to her husband.

The Opposite Sex

From [2] and [3], Marion cannot be an only daughter and have a sister; so Marion is a male. Then, from [3], Marion is Carmen's brother.

From [2], Marion's sister is either Evelyn or Leslie. Suppose Evelyn is Marion's sister; then, from [1], Carmen is Leslie's only son. But, from previous reasoning, Marion is Carmen's brother; so Marion would also be Leslie's son. This situation contradicts [1]. So Leslie, not Evelyn, is Marion's sister.

Then, from [1], Evelyn is Leslie's only son.

It is now known that Marion and Evelyn are males and Leslie is a female. So, from [4], *Leslie is the opposite sex from each of the others* and Carmen is a male.

In summary: Leslie is a female, Marion and Carmen are her brothers, and Evelyn is her son.

Truth Day

From [1], Philip's declarations in [3] and [5] cannot both be false; otherwise he tells the truth on more than one of the days of the week. From [1] and the fact that the declarations in [3] through [5] were made on consecutive days, Philip's declarations in [3] and [5] cannot both be true; otherwise he tells the truth on more than one of the days of the week. So either Philip's declaration in [3] is the only true one or his declaration in [5] is the only true one.

Suppose his declaration in [3] is the only true one. Then, from his false declaration in [5], he made the declaration in [3] on a Wednesday or a Friday. Then, from [2], his false declaration in [4] was made on a Thursday or a Saturday. This situation is impossible.

So his declaration in [5] is the only true one. Then, from his false declaration in [3], he made the declaration in [5] on a Monday or a Tuesday. Then, from [2], his false declaration in [4] was made on a Sunday or a Monday. His declaration in [4] could not have been made on a Sunday; otherwise his declaration in [4] would be true. So his declaration in [4] was made on a Monday.

Then, from [2], his true declaration in [5] was made on a Tuesday and *Philip tells the truth on Tuesday.*

The Murderer in the Hotel

From [2], there was only one murderer. So either one hypothesis of [4] and [5] is false or both hypotheses in [4] and [5] are false.

Case I. Suppose both hypotheses in [4] and [5] are false. Then the murderer and the victim stayed in rooms that bordered on the same number of rooms (from [4]), and that were the same size (from [5]). This situation is impossible, from [1].

Case II. Suppose the hypothesis in [4] is true and the hypothesis in [5] is false. Then the murderer and the victim stayed in rooms that bordered on different numbers of rooms (from [4]), and that were the same size (from [5]). Then, from [1], either: (a) Arlene or Farley was the victim and the other was the murderer, (b) Brenda or Daniel was the victim and the other was the murderer, or (c) Cheryl or

Emmett was the victim and the other was the murderer. From [4], a is impossible and, from [3], b and c are impossible.

Case III. So the hypothesis in [5] is true and the hypothesis in [4] is false. Then the murderer and the victim stayed in rooms that bordered on the same number of rooms (from [4]), and that were different in size (from [5]). Then, from [1], either: (d) Arlene or Daniel was the victim and the other was the murderer, (e) Brenda or Emmett was the victim and the other was the murderer, or (f) Cheryl or Farley was the victim and the other was the murderer. From [5], f is impossible and, from [3], e is impossible. Then d is correct and, from [5], *Daniel was the murderer.* So Arlene was the victim.

The Three Groups

Exactly two of the three hypotheses in [2], [3], and [4] must be false. So, because a hypothetical statement is true when the hypothesis in it is false, at least two of the declarations in [2], [3], and [4] must be true.

Case I. Only the declaration in [2] is false. Then Anita's hypothesis is true and her conclusion is false. Then, from [1], each person is a Normal.

Case II. Only the declaration in [3] is false. Then Beryl's hypothesis is true and her conclusion is false. Then, from [1], Beryl is a Normal. (If Beryl is a Fibber, then someone else must be a Fibber, which is impossible.) Then either Anita and Chloe are both Trusties, Anita is a Trusty and Chloe is a Normal, or Chloe is a Trusty and Anita is a Normal.

Case III. Only the declaration in [4] is false. Then Chloe's hypothesis is true and her conclusion is false. Then, from

[1], Chloe is a Normal and either Anita or Beryl is a Fibber. This situation is impossible, from [1].

Case IV. The declarations in [2], [3], and [4] are all true. Then, because exactly one of their hypotheses is true, one of their conclusions is true. Then at least one person is a Fibber. This situation is impossible, from [1].

In summary: Anita is a Trusty or a Normal, Beryl is a Normal, and Chloe is a Trusty or a Normal. So *you know Beryl's group*.

Code Word

S must be 1. Then D (under L) is greater than 5. If D is 6, then L is 0; but then A is 0 or 1, which is impossible. If D is 7, then L is 0 and A is 2. If D is 8, then L is 2; then A is 3. If D is 9, then L is 2 or 3 and A is 3 or 4. So either:

Case	S	D	L	A
i	1	7	0	2
ii	1	8	2	3
iii	1	9	2	3
iv	1	9	2	4
v	1	9	3	4

If 1 was carried from D to E, then N would have to be 9 and D (over A) would have to be 6 more than A. So Case iii is eliminated. Then E (over N) is 1 more than N. So E is not 0.

E is not 1. If E is 2, then N is 1; so E is not 2. If E is 3, then N is 2; so E is not 3.

So E is greater than 3. Then 1 was carried from L to I (or D − L = 6). So Cases i and iv are eliminated.

If E is 4, then N is 3; so E is not 4. If E is 5, then I is 1; so

E is not 5. If E is 7, then I is 3; so E is not 7. If E is 8, then I is 4; so E is not 8. If E is 9, then N is 8; so E is not 9. So E is 6.

Then I is 2 and N is 5. So Case ii is eliminated (because I is 2) and Case v is the correct one.

In summary: Case	S	D	L	A	E	I	N
v	1	9	3	4	6	2	5

Then *the word that represents 3651 is LENS.*

The Winning Mark

1	2	3
4	5	6
7	8	9

Let a number in each square as shown indicate the location of a mark. Then, from [3], the seventh mark must be placed in square 3 where, from [2], it wins for X or O; or be placed in square 9 where, from [2], it wins for X. So, from [3], the sixth mark must have been placed in a line already containing two of the opponent's marks: either in square 2 or in square 7; otherwise, either X or O would have been placed in square 3 or X would have been placed in square 9. So before the sixth mark was placed in a square the situation was either:

O		
O	X	
X	X	

Case I

O	O	
O	X	
	X	

Case II

In Case I an X must be the fifth mark, from [1]. But none of the Xs could be the fifth mark because, from [3], as the fifth mark: the X in square 5 would have been placed in square 9, the X in square 7 would have been placed in square 2, and the X in square 8 would have been placed in square 3. So Case I is not the correct situation.

Then Case II is the correct situation and, from [1], O was the fifth mark. Then, from [1], the seventh mark will be O and, from [2], O *wins the game.*

Which O was the fifth mark can be determined from [3]. As the fifth mark: the O in square 2 would have been placed in square 7 and the O in square 4 would have been placed in square 3. So the fifth mark was the O in square 1.

A Big Party

From [1],

number of men	+	number of women	= 14
+		+	
number of boys	+	number of girls	= 17
=		=	
12		19	

So, keeping the spatial relationship indicated, one gets either:

0 + 14	1 + 13	2 + 12	3 + 11
+ +	+ +	+ +	+ +
12 + 5,	11 + 6,	10 + 7,	9 + 8,

4 + 10	5 + 9	6 + 8	7 + 7
+ +	+	+ +	+ +
8 + 9,	7 + 10,	6 + 11,	5 + 12,

$$
\begin{array}{llll}
8+\ 6 & 9+\ 5 & 10+\ 4 & 11+\ 3 \\
+\quad + & +\quad + & +\quad + & +\quad + \\
4+13, & 3+14, & 2+15, & 1+16,
\end{array}
$$

$$
\text{or} \quad
\begin{array}{l}
12+\ 2 \\
+\quad + \\
0+17.
\end{array}
$$

Then, from [2], one compares the product of the top two numbers with the product of the bottom two numbers in each case; the difference between the products should be one of the numbers multiplied to get the smaller product. Trial and error reveals that 9 + 5 is the correct case: 9 × 5 = 3 × 14 + 3   +   +
                                  3 + 14

or 9 × 5 = 3 × 15. So *the speaker is a girl.*

This puzzle can also be solved by using algebra, as follows. Let m be the number of male adults. Then, from [1],

$$
\begin{array}{ll}
m+14-m & = \text{number of adults} \\
+\quad + \\
12-m+m+5 & = \text{number of children} \\
=\qquad = \\
\text{number} \quad \text{number} \\
\text{of males} \quad \text{of females}
\end{array}
$$

Then, from [2], the speaker is either a
(I) man: $(m+1)\times(14-m) = (12-m)\times(m+5)$ or (II) woman: $(m)\times(14-m+1) = (12-m)\times(m+5)$ or (III) boy: $(m)\times(14-m) = (12-m+1)\times(m+5)$ or (IV) girl: $(m)\times(14-m) = (12-m)\times(m+5+1)$.

Attempting to solve each equation in turn, one finds that m can be a whole number only in IV:

I.
$$(m+1)\times(14-m) = (12-m)\times(m+5)$$
$$14m-m+14-m^2 = 12m-5m+60-m^2$$
$$13m+14 = 7m+60$$
$$6m = 46 \qquad \text{impossible}$$

II.
$$(m)\times(15-m) = (12-m)\times(m+5)$$
$$15m-m^2 = 12m-5m+60-m^2$$
$$15m = 7m+60$$
$$8m = 60 \qquad \text{impossible}$$

III.
$$(m)\times(14-m) = (13-m)\times(m+5)$$
$$14m-m^2 = 13m-5m+65-m^2$$
$$14m = 8m+65$$
$$6m = 65 \qquad \text{impossible}$$

IV.
$$(m)\times(14-m) = (12-m)\times(m+6)$$
$$14m-m^2 = 12m-6m+72-m^2$$
$$14m = 6m+72$$
$$8m = 72$$
$$m = 9$$

So m + 14 − m becomes 9 + 5 and *the speaker is a girl.*
$$+ \qquad + \qquad\qquad + \qquad +$$
$$12-m + m+5 \qquad\quad 3 + 14$$

The Tennis Game

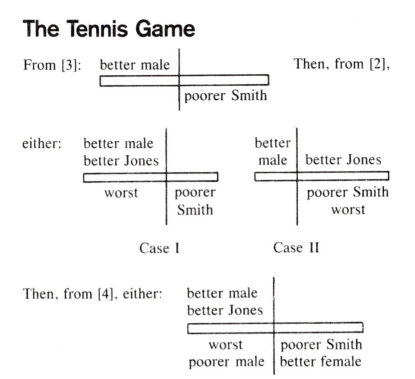

From [3]: better male
poorer Smith

Then, from [2],

either: better male
better Jones
worst | poorer Smith

better male | better Jones
poorer Smith worst

Case I   Case II

Then, from [4], either: better male
better Jones
worst poorer male | poorer Smith better female

Case I

better male | better Jones
better female | poorer Smith worst poorer male

Then, from [1], either:

Case II

better male better Jones Mr. Jones	Mrs. Jones	better male Mr. Jones	better Jones Mrs. Jones
worst poorer male Mr. Smith	poorer Smith better female Mrs. Smith	better female Mrs. Smith	poorer Smith worst poorer male Mr. Smith

Case I	Case II

Then, in Case I, Mr. Smith is the worst player and Mrs. Smith is the poorer Smith player. This situation is impossible. So Case I is not a correct case.

Then Case II is a correct case. Then the worst player is Mr. Smith, the better male player is Mr. Jones, the better Jones player is Mrs. Jones, and the better female player is Mrs. Smith. So *the best player is Mrs. Smith.*

Note: If the better male player is placed in the upper right instead of the upper left of the diagram, then the placement of the players will be

Mrs. Jones	Mr. Jones
Mr. Smith	Mrs. Smith

; but the

order of playing abilities remains the same.

Multiples of 7

From [1] and [2], each number represented by AB, AC, BE, CF, EG, and FG is either 00, 07, 14, 21, 28, 35, 42, 49, 56, 63, 70, 77, 84, 91, or 98. Then, from [3] and the listed numbers, A must be either 0, 2, 4, 7, or 9 and G must be either 0, 1, 4, 7, or 8. So:

	If A is	Then B or C is
Case I	0 or 7	0 or 7
Case II	2 or 9	1 or 8
Case III	4	2 or 9

Then E or F is	If G is	
0 or 7	0 or 7	Case i
2 or 9	1 or 8	Case ii
1 or 8	4	Case iii

Case I, II, or III must coexist with Case i, ii, or iii so that BE is a multiple of 7.

Case I. If B is 0 or 7, then E must be 0 or 7. Then either 00, 07, 70, or 77 occurs twice among AB, AC, EG, and FG. This situation is impossible, from [3].

Case II. If B is 1 or 8, then E must be 4. This situation is impossible because neither Case i, ii, nor iii allows E to be 4.

Case III. So this case is the correct one. Then B is 2 or 9. Then E is 1 or 8. Then Case iii coexists with Case III.

So A is 4 and G is 4. Then 1 must be carried to G when ADG is divided by 7. So D must be 1 more than 2 which is 3. Then *ADG must represent 434.*

The coexistence of Cases III and iii results in these four possible arrangements of the digits:

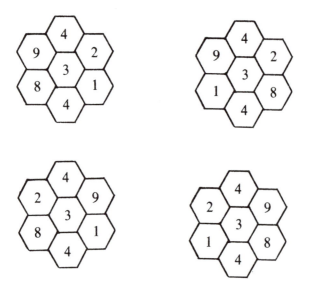

In each arrangement, BDF and CDE are multiples of 7.

Harry Will Marry

From [1a] and [3a], either (A represents April, B represents Bette, C represents Clare, H represents hazel eyes, h represents no hazel eyes):

Case I		
A	B	C
H	H	h

Case II		
A	B	C
h	h	H

Then, from [1b] and [2a], either (R represents red hair, r represents no red hair):

Case Ia		
A	B	C
H	H	h
R	r	R

Case Ib		
A	B	C
H	H	h
r	R	r

Case IIa		
A	B	C
h	h	H
R	r	R

Case IIb		
A	B	C
h	h	H
r	R	r

From [2b] and [3b], either: (i) Clare is the only one of the three who is slender, or (ii) Clare is the only one of the three who is not slender. From [4], neither i nor ii is possible in Cases Ia and IIb (one woman cannot have exactly one characteristic at the same time that another woman has exactly two characteristics because Harry will marry only one woman). So, from [4], either (S represents slender, s represents not slender):

Case Ib		
A	B	C
H	H	h
r	R	r
S	S	s

Case IIa		
A	B	C
h	h	H
R	r	R
s	s	S

Then, from [4a], Harry will marry Clare in Case Ib and, from [4b], Harry will marry Clare in Case IIa. So, in either case, *Harry will marry Clare.*

The President

Suppose [4a] is true. Then, from [1] and [2], [3b] is true. Then, from [1] and [2], [4b] is true. Then, from [2], Curtis is the President. Then, from [1], [5a] and [5b] are both false. Then, from [1] and because [5a] is false, [3a] is false. But [3a] cannot be false because the President does belong to a different group from each of the other two (from [1]). So [4a] is not true but false.

With [4a] false, suppose [4b] is true and Blaine is the President. Then, because Blaine is the President, [3b] is false and [5b] is true. Then, because Blaine is the President and is an Alternator (from [1]), [3a] is false. Then [5a] can be neither true nor false. So, with [4b] true, Blaine is not the President.

With [4a] false, suppose [4b] is true and Curtis is the President. Then, because Curtis is the President, [3b] is true and [5b] is false. Then, because [4a] and [5b] are false, [5a] is true. Then, because Blaine and Curtis are both Alternators (from [1]) and Curtis is the President, [3a] is false. Then [5a] is false. Then [5a] is both true and false. This situation is impossible. So, with [4b] true, Curtis is not the President.

Then, with [4a] false, [4b] is not true but false. Then, *Aubrey is the President.*

Then [4a] and [4b] are false, and [3b] and [5b] are true. Suppose [3a] is false. Then, because there must be another Alternator along with Aubrey, [5a] is false. But [5a] cannot be false. So [3a] is true. Then, because there must not be another Truthteller, [5a] is false. That [5a] is false is confirmed by the result.

In summary: Aubrey is a Truthteller and the President, Blaine is a Falsifier, and Curtis is an Alternator who first lied and then told the truth.

Apartments

From [2], there is only one landlord. So no more than one of the conclusions in [3] through [6] is true.

Suppose no conclusion is true in [3] through [6]. Then each hypothesis in [3] through [6] is false. Then, from false hypotheses in [3] and [5], Blake's apartment is between Clark's and Doyle's. Then both hypotheses in [4] and [6] cannot be false. So this situation is impossible.

So exactly one conclusion is true in [3] through [6]. Then, because the other three conclusions are false, the hypotheses associated with the three conclusions are false. Then, because all the hypotheses cannot be false, the hypothesis associated with the true conclusion is true.

Suppose the hypothesis in [3] is the only true hypothesis. Then from [3], Avery lives in apartment a. From [1] and because the hypothesis in [6] is false, this situation is impossible.

Suppose the hypothesis in [4] is the only true hypothesis. Then, from [4], Doyle lives in apartment d. From [1] and because the hypothesis in [6] is false, this situation is impossible.

Suppose the hypothesis in [6] is the only true hypothesis. Then, from [6], Blake lives in apartment b. Then, from [1] and the false hypotheses in [3] and [5], Avery lives in apartment d. From [1] and because the hypothesis in [4] is false, this situation is impossible.

So the hypothesis in [5] is the only true one. Then, from [5], *Clark is the landlord.*

From [5], Clark lives in apartment c. So, from [1] and the false hypotheses in [4] and [6], Blake lives in apartment d. Then, from [1] and the false hypothesis in [6], Doyle lives in apartment a and Avery lives in apartment b. With this arrangement, the hypothesis in [3] is false, as it should be.

Murderer's Occupation

From [8], as many as fourteen correct choices are possible (only one for occupation, two each for weight and

235

smoking habits, and three each for the other particulars) and as few as eight correct choices are possible (three for sex and one each for the other particulars) in [1] through [6]. From [7], the number of correct choices is a multiple of six. So the number of correct choices is twelve, each detective getting two. The following reasoning uses [1] through [6].

The murderer could not be both 63 to 66 inches tall and 20 to 30 years old; otherwise, one detective would have gotten three particulars correct, including sex. The murderer could not be either 63 to 66 inches tall or 20 to 30 years old; otherwise, the number of correct choices would be less than twelve (one for height, one for age, one for occupation, three for sex, and at most two each for weight and smoking habits). So either the murderer is 63 to 66 inches tall or the murderer is 20 to 30 years old, but not both.

Then (because the murderer is either 63 to 66 inches tall or 20 to 30 years old, but not both) two detectives are correct about the weight—110 to 130 pounds or 130 to 150 pounds—and two detectives are correct about the smoking habits—cigarette smoker or cigar smoker; otherwise, the number of correct choices would be less than twelve (four for height and age, one for occupation, three for sex, and less than four for weight and smoking habits).

If the murderer is 63 to 66 inches tall, then the murderer cannot be a male; otherwise, the murderer would be a cigarette smoker or a cigar smoker (already established) and some detective would have more than two correct choices. Then the murderer is a female. Using the fact that each detective got two correct choices, one finds: first, the murderer is a cigar smoker; next, the murderer weighs 110 to 130 pounds; next, no correct age choice is possible. So the murderer is not 63 to 66 inches tall.

Then the murderer is 20 to 30 years old. Then the murderer cannot be a male; otherwise, the murderer would weigh either 110 to 130 pounds or 130 to 150 pounds (already established) and some detective would have more than two correct choices. Then the murderer is a female. Then, from [4], *the murderer is a draper* and a cigar smoker (no other particulars are left in [4]). Then, from [1], the murderer weighs 110 to 130 pounds (no other particular is left in [1]). Then, from [3], the murderer is 69 to 72 inches tall (no other particular is left in [3]).

The Owner of the Table

From [1] and [6], either (M_1 is man, W_1 is woman, $\bigcirc$ is owner of table):

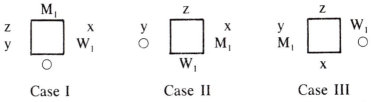

Case I   Case II   Case III

Case I. If x is a man, then y is a man; otherwise z's position contradicts [6]. If x is a woman, then y is a woman; otherwise W_1's position contradicts [6].

Case II. If x is a man, then $\bigcirc$ is a man; otherwise y's position contradicts [6]. If x is a woman, then $\bigcirc$ is a woman: otherwise M_1's position contradicts [6].

Case III. If x is a man, then y is a man; otherwise z's position contradicts [6]. But if x is a man and y is a man, then W_1's position contradicts [6], from [2]. So this situation is impossible. If x is a woman, then $\bigcirc$ is a woman; otherwise M_1's position contradicts [6]. But if x is a woman and $\bigcirc$ is a woman, then x's position contradicts [6], from [2]. So this situation is impossible.

So either (M_1 is first man, M_2 is second man, etc.):

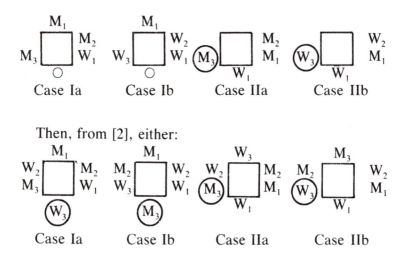

Case Ia   Case Ib   Case IIa   Case IIb

Then, from [2], either:

Case Ia   Case Ib   Case IIa   Case IIb

Then, from [5] followed by [4] followed by [2], either (W_C is Cecile, M_D is Dudley, M_E is Edward, and M_F is Foster):

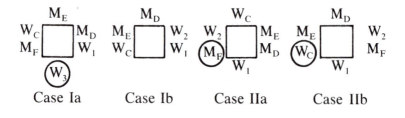

Case Ia   Case Ib   Case IIa   Case IIb

Then, from [3], Cases Ia, Ib, and IIa are impossible and Case IIb is correct. Then *Cecile owned the table.* From [3], W_1 is Althea; then, from [2], W_2 is Blythe.

Family Murder

Suppose Statements I and II are both true. Then, from [1], a different woman made each one. Then, from [1], a man made Statement III. Then, from [1] and [2], the victim is a man. Then Statement III is true. This situation contradicts [3], so it is impossible. Then, from [3], either Statement I or Statement II is false and Statement III is true.

Suppose the true Statement III was made by a woman. Then, from [1] and [2], Statements I and II were each made by a different man. Then both Statements I and II are false. This situation contradicts [3], so it is impossible. Then the true Statement III was made by a man. Then the victim was a man. Then, from [1] and [2], one of Statements I and II was made by Alice and the other was made by Alice's mother; and either Alice's brother or Alice's son is the victim.

Suppose Statement II is the false statement. (A) If Alice's brother is the victim, Alice's mother could not have made a true Statement I; so Alice's mother made a false Statement II and Alice is the murderer. But then Alice would have to have made a true Statement I. This situation is impossible. (B) If Alice's son is the victim, Alice could not have made a true Statement I; so Alice made a false Statement II and Alice's son is the murderer. This situation is impossible. So, from A and B, Statement II is not the false statement.

Then, from [3], Statement I is the false statement. (C) If Alice's brother is the victim, Alice's mother made a true Statement II. Then Alice is not the murderer and Alice made a false Statement I. Then Alice's son is not the murderer. Then Alice's mother is the murderer. (D) If Alice's son is the victim, Alice made a true Statement II. Then Alice's mother made a false Statement I. Then neither Alice nor Alice's brother is the murderer. Then Alice's mother is the murderer.

Then, from C and D, *Alice's mother is the murderer.* (Note: It is not possible to tell who made each statement and who is the victim.)

The Dart Game

From [1] and [2], any of six values was scored by a dart. Then, from [4], the men either scored two different values each or one man scored only one value.

If the men each scored two different values, then one man scored five 1s, from [1] and [3]. Then, from [1] and [2], each total score ends in 5 because the man who scored the five 1s scored four of a value that ends in 5 or 0. So a second man scored all the 5s (from [5], this man is Arnold) and the third man scored all the 25s. Then Buford could not have scored the five 1s because, from [3], he would have scored four 10s making his total score less than 100; this situation contradicts the assumption started with and [1]. Then Conrad scored the five 1s and his total score was either 205 (five 1s and four 50s) or 405 (five 1s and four 100s), from [1] and [2]. But then Buford, who scored all the 10s (from [5]) and all the 25s (from previous reasoning), could not have scored either total. So each man did not score two different values.

Then one man scored only one value. Then, from [1], [2], and [4], at least five different values were scored. The single value scored by one man could not have been 1 or 100 because a total score of 9 or 900 could not be scored in any other way, from [4]. The single value could not be 5, totaling 45, because at least one 50 or one 100 was scored. The single value could not be 10, totaling 90, because then (from [1] through [4]): there would be no 100s, a second man would have to score one 50 and eight 5s, and the third man would have to score 90 with five 1s and four 25s; this situation is impossible. The single value could not be 50, totaling 450, because (from [1] and [4]) a second man would have some 100s and the total of 450 could not be scored by the third man with only values less than 50. So, from [1], the single value was 25.

Then, from [5], Conrad scored all the 25s. Then, from [3],

the total score of each man was 225. For each man's score to end in 5, one man has to have 25s, a second man has to have 5s, and the third man has to have five 1s (from [1], [3], and [4]). So, from [5], Buford scored five 1s. Then, from [5], Buford scored two 10s and two 100s as well. So *Buford scored all the 100s*. Then, from [1] and [4], Arnold scored five 5s and four 50s.

Hotel Rooms

From [2] through [6], (X) the man who lied occupied the same size room as another man. From [2] and [7]: (i) If the man who lied occupied a room that bordered on four other rooms, then that room bordered on two rooms occupied by men and two rooms occupied by women. (ii) If the man who lied occupied a room that bordered on three other rooms, then that room bordered on one room occupied by a man and two rooms occupied by women. (iii) If the man who lied occupied a room that bordered on two other rooms, then that room bordered on two rooms occupied by women.

The following reasoning uses [2].

Case I. (a) Suppose the man who lied occupied room C. Then, from i, a woman occupied room A. This situation contradicts X, so it is impossible. (b) Suppose the man who lied occupied room F. Then, from i, a woman occupied room D and, from X, a man occupied room E. Then, from [7], a man occupied room C; otherwise room E, occupied by a man, bordered on two rooms occupied by women, contradicting [7]. Then, from [1], women occupied rooms A and B. But room C, occupied by a man, borders on two rooms occupied by women. This situation contradicts [7], so it is impossible.

Case II. (c) Suppose the man who lied occupied room B. Then, from X, a man occupied room D. Then, from [7], rooms C and E were not both occupied by women; otherwise room D, occupied by a man, bordered on two rooms occupied by women. So room C or E was occupied by a man, from [1], and rooms A and F were both occupied by women. Then, from [7], room E was not occupied by a man; otherwise room E bordered on two rooms occupied by women, from [1], contradicting [7]. So room E was occupied by a woman. Then room C, occupied by a man, from [1], borders on two rooms occupied by women. This situation contradicts [7], so it is impossible. (d) Suppose the man who lied occupied room E. Then, from X, a man occupied room F. Then, from ii, women occupied rooms C and D. Then room F, occupied by a man, borders on two rooms occupied by women, from [1]. This situation contradicts [7], so it is impossible.

Case III. (e) Suppose the man who lied occupied room D. Then, from iii, women occupied rooms C and E and, from X, a man occupied room B. Then room B, occupied by a man, borders on two rooms occupied by women, from [1]. This situation contradicts [7], so it is impossible. (f) The man who lied, then, occupied room A. Then, from iii, women occupied rooms B and F and, from X, a man occupied room C; from [4], this man was Brian. Then, from [7], room E was not occupied by a man; otherwise room E bordered on two rooms occupied by women, from [1], contradicting [7]. So room E was occupied by a woman. Then room D was occupied by a man, from [1]; from [5], this man was Clyde. So, from [3], *Arden lied*.

The Numbered Discs

From [1], [2], and [6], this axiom holds: When a woman saw two 2s on the other two women, she knew she had either a 2 or a 3 on her forehead.

From [1] through [5], as each woman was asked in turn to name the number on her forehead, each woman's reasoning in turn went like this:

First woman:	I have a 2 or a 3 [from axiom].
Second woman:	I have a 2 or a 3 [from axiom]. If I have a 2, first woman wouldn't know whether she had a 2 or a 3. If I have a 3, first woman wouldn't know whether she had a 1 or a 2. So I don't know whether I have a 2 or a 3.
Third woman:	I have a 2 or a 3 [from axiom]. If I have a 2, first woman wouldn't know whether she had a 2 or a 3 and second woman wouldn't know whether she had a 2 or a 3. [See above.] If I have a 3, first woman wouldn't know whether she had a 1 or a 2 and second woman wouldn't know whether she had a 1 or a 2; second woman would reason: if I have a 1, first woman wouldn't know whether she had a 2 or a 3 and if I have a 2, first woman wouldn't know whether she had a 1 or a 2. So I don't know whether I have a 2 or a 3.
First woman:	I have a 2 or a 3. If I have a 3, second woman would know she had a 2: second woman would know she didn't have a 1 because otherwise I would have known I had a 3; second woman would know she didn't have a 3 because the total is 6 or 7. Second woman didn't know she had a 2; so I have a 2.
Second woman:	I have a 2 or a 3. If I have a 3, third woman would know she had a 2: third woman would know she didn't have a 1 because otherwise I would have known I had a 3; third woman would know she didn't have a 3 because the total is 6 or 7.

243

	Third woman didn't know she had a 2; so I have a 2.
Third woman:	I have a 2 or a 3. If I have a 2, each of first and second women would know the second time around she had a 2. [See above.] If I have a 3, first woman would know she had a 2: first woman would know the first time around she had a 1 or a 2; first woman would know the second time around she didn't have a 1 because otherwise I would have known I had a 3. If I have a 3, second woman would know she had a 2: second woman would know the first time around she had a 1 or a 2 [see third woman's reasoning first time around]; second woman would know the second time around she didn't have a 1 because otherwise I would have known I had a 3. So I still don't know whether I have a 2 or a 3.

(At this point no more information can be obtained by the third woman.)

Then *the third woman asked failed to name her number.*

Finishing First

Prediction [1] has three first-through-fifth-position entrants, prediction [4] has three first-through-fifth-position entrants, and predictions [1] and [4] have exactly one entrant—Bea—in common. So all five first-through-fifth-position entrants are in [1] and [4], and Bea is one of them.

Then any entrant not in [1] and [4] was not among the first-through-fifth-position entrants. So Hal and Jan are eliminated.

Suppose Don was one of the five first-through-fifth-position entrants. Then, because Hal was not one of the five and from [2], each of Flo, Guy, and Eve was not one of the five. Then, from [5], each of Ada and Cal was one of the five. From [1], this situation is impossible because Bea was one of the five and Don was supposed to be one of the five. So Don was not one of the five.

Then, from [2] and [5], either Ada or Cal was one of the five. Then, from [1], Eve was one of the five because Bea was one of the five and Don was not.

Then, from [2], each of Flo and Guy was not one of the five because Eve was one of the five and each of Hal and Don was not.

Then, from [4], each of Ken and Ida was one of the five because Eve was one of the five and each of Flo and Guy was not.

Then, from [3], Cal was not one of the five because each of Ida and Eve was.

Then, from [1] or [5], Ada was one of the five because six of the eleven entrants have been eliminated.

In summary: Bea, Eve, Ken, Ida, and Ada were the five first-through-fifth-position entrants. So, from [3] and [5], Ada finished fourth. Then, from [1], Bea finished second and Eve finished fifth. Then, from [4], Ken finished third. So *Ida finished first.*

The Lead in the Play

From [2] and [6], dressing room C bordered on a man's dressing room and a woman's dressing room. So (i) dressing rooms B and D were occupied by a man and a woman. Again, from [2] and [6], dressing room A bordered on a man's dressing room and a woman's dressing room. So (ii) dressing rooms B and E were occupied by a man and a woman. Then, from i and ii, (y) dressing rooms D and E were both occupied by men or both occupied by women.

From [1] and [2], there were two men and two pairs of siblings of opposite sex in the dressing rooms. Then, from [3], (z) dressing rooms A and C or dressing rooms D and E were occupied by a man and a woman. Then, from y and z, (I) dressing rooms A and C were occupied by a man and a woman.

From [1], there were only two men; so, from y and I, (II) dressing rooms D and E were both occupied by women. So, three women and one man being accounted for in I and II, dressing room B was occupied by a man.

Then, from [2] and [5], the man who occupied dressing room B was not Tyrone. Then, from [1], Tyrone's son occupied dressing room B; and, from [1] and [3], Tyrone and his sister occupied dressing rooms A and C, and one of them was the lead in the play. Then, from [2] and [5], the dressing rooms were occupied in one of the following ways (T represents Tyrone):

T	T's son	T's sis-ter
	T's daugh-	

Case I

T's sis-ter	T's son		T
T's daughter			

Case II

From previous reasoning, the lead was either Tyrone or his sister. From [1], Tyrone's mother occupied dressing room E in Case I or dressing room D in Case II. In either case, *Tyrone's sister was the lead*, from [4].

The Center Card

From [1], any corner card borders on just two cards, any mid-edge card borders on just three cards, and the center card borders on just four cards. From [2] and [5], each of two aces borders on a queen; from [3] and [5], each of two kings borders on a queen: and, from [4] and [5], each of two queens borders on the same jack or two different jacks. So the queens border on at least five different cards.

There are three ways for two cards to be bordered on by a total of five cards:

Case I

	•	X
	•	•
•	X	•

The two cards (Xs) are a corner card and a mid-edge card with each of the five cards (dots) bordering on only one of them.

Case II

•	X	•
	•	
•	X	•

The two cards (Xs) are both mid-edge cards with one of the five cards (dots) bordering on both of them.

Case III

	•	
•	X	•
•	X	•

The two cards (Xs) are the center card and a mid-edge card bordering on each other with each of the five cards (dots) bordering on only one of them.

If there are only two queens (Xs), then: Case I does not apply because two jacks (dots) as well as two aces (dots) and two kings (dots) would be necessary; Case II does not apply because no ace (dot) could border on a king (dot) as required by [2]; and Case III does not apply because the two queens could not border on the same jack (dot) as well as two aces (dots) and two kings (dots).

So there are three queens. Then five cards border on two jacks (Xs): three queens (dots), from [4]; and two kings (dots), from [3] and [5]. Then in Cases I, II, and III the unmarked cards are aces. Then: Case I does not apply, from [2]; Case II does not apply, from [3]. So Case III applies and *a jack is in the center*.

From previous reasoning, the Xs are jacks and the unmarked cards are aces (J represents jack and A represents ace):

Then, because every king borders on a queen (from [3]), the top dot is not a king; so the top dot is a queen. Then, because every ace borders on a king (from [2]), the dots in the second row are kings. Then, because there are three queens, the remaining dots are queens.

Dogs and Cats

If the conclusion in [2] is true, then the hypothesis in [1] is false; then the declarations in [1] and [2] are both true, contradicting [5]. So (i) the conclusion in [2] is false.

If Angus does not have a dog, then the hypotheses in [1] and [3] are false; then the declarations in [1] and [3] are both true, contradicting [5]. So Angus has a dog. Then, because the conclusion in [2] is false, both Angus and Duane have dogs. So (ii) the hypothesis in [1] is true.

If the conclusion in [3] is true, then the hypothesis in [4] is false; then the declarations in [3] and [4] are both true, contradicting [5]. So (iii) the conclusion in [3] is false.

If Basil does not have a cat, then the hypotheses in [2] and [4] are false; then the declarations in [2] and [4] are both true, contradicting [5]. So Basil has a cat. Then, because the conclusion in [3] is false, both Basil and Duane have cats. So (iv) the hypothesis in [4] is true.

Suppose (X) neither Basil nor Craig has a dog. Then the hypothesis in [3] is false and the conclusion in [4] is true. So the declarations in [3] and [4] are both true, contradicting [5]. So X is not true.

Suppose (Y) Basil has a dog and Craig does not. Then the conclusion in [1] is true and the hypothesis in [3] is false. So the declarations in [1] and [3] are both true, contradicting [5]. So Y is not true.

Suppose (Z) Craig has a dog and Basil does not. Then the conclusions in [1] and [4] are true. So the declarations in [1] and [4] are both true, contradicting [5]. So Z is not true.

Then (because X, Y, and Z are not true) both Basil and Craig have dogs. Then (v) the conclusion in [1] is false.

Because Basil and Duane both have dogs, (vi) the conclusion in [4] is false.

Because Angus and Craig both have dogs, (vii) the hypothesis in [3] is true.

Then: from ii and v, the declaration in [1] is false; from iii and vii, the declaration in [3] is false; and, from iv and vi, the declaration in [4] is false. So, from [5], the declaration in [2] is true and *Basil is telling the truth*. Then, from i, the hypothesis in [2] is false. Then, because Basil has a cat, Craig does not have a cat.

Whether or not Angus has a cat cannot be determined.

The Omitted Age

From [1], let the required digits be A, B, C, D, E, F, and G as in

	a A	b B
c C	D	E
d F	G	

Then, from [3], either:

Case I	Case II	Case III	Case IV
ADG	ADG	ADG	ADG
+ AB	+ BE	+ CF	+ FG
CDE	CDE	CDE	CDE

Case I. In the middle column, A is 9 or 0. Then, from [2], A is 9. Then C is more than 9 in the left column. This situation is impossible. So Case I is not a correct case.

Case II. B is 9 or 0. Then, from [2], B is 9. Then 1 was carried from the right column. But G must be 0, so 1 could not be carried from the right column. This situation is impossible. So Case II is not a correct case.

Case III. In the middle column, C is 9 or 0. Then, from [2], C is 9. But, from [3], AB ; so C in CDE could not be

$$
\begin{array}{r}
BE \\
CF \\
+ FG \\
\hline
CDE
\end{array}
$$

greater than 3. This situation is impossible. So Case III is not a correct case.

Case IV. So this case must be a correct case and, from [3], *Blanche's age was omitted from a down.* F is 9 or 0. Then, from [2], F is 9. Then 1 was carried from the right column and 1 was carried from the middle column. Because 1 was carried from the right column, G is greater than 4. Because 1 was carried from the middle column, C is 1 more than A. Because Case IV is correct and from [3], AB Then A is 1 and C is 2, or A is 2 and C

$$
\begin{array}{r}
BE \\
+ CF \\
\hline
ADG
\end{array}
$$

is 3. But, if A is 2 and C is 3 in the middle column, then A cannot be 2 in ADG. So A is 1 and C is 2. Because F is 9 and G is greater than 4, B + F + G in the right column of AB must be 20 (B + F + G must end in 0).

$$
\begin{array}{r}
BE \\
CF \\
+ FG
\end{array}
$$

Then, because F is 9, B + G is 11. Then, because B + G is 11 and G is greater than 4, B is 6 or less. Because A is 1 and C is 2 and F is 9, A + B + C + F is at least 18; so B is 6 or more. Because B is 6 or less and 6 or more, B is 6. Then, because B + G is 11, G is 5. Then D is 0 in

AB and E is 0 in ADG. Then the completed puzzle is

BE	+ FG
CF	CDE
+ FG	
CDE	

	a 1	b 6
c 2	0	0
d 9	5	

The Hats

Of two black hats and two white hats, let X represent one color hat and let Y represent the other color hat. Then from [1], [2], and [6], either:

	First man wore	Second man wore	Third man wore	Fourth man wore
Case I	X	Y	X	Y
Case II	X	Y	Y	X
Case III	X	X	Y	Y

From [1] and [2], this axiom holds: When a man saw two (a) black (b) white hats on two of the other three men, he knew he wore either a red hat or a (a) white (b) black hat.

From [1] through [5], as each man was asked in turn the color of the hat on his head, each man's reasoning in turn went like this (R represents a red hat):

Case I

First man: I have R or X [from axiom].

Second man: I have R or Y [from axiom].

Third man: I have R or X [from axiom]. If I have R, first man would know he had X [from axiom]; he didn't know, so I have X.

Fourth man: I have R or X [from axiom]. If I have R,

	second man would know he had Y [from axiom]; he didn't know, so I have Y.
First man:	I have R or X. If I have R, third man would know he had X [from axiom]; then fourth man would know he had Y because third man knew he had X. If I have X, each of the third and fourth men would also know what color he had [see above]. So I still don't know whether I have R or X.
Second man:	I have R or Y. If I have R, fourth man would know he had Y [from axiom]; and third man would know he had X because first man didn't know he had X. If I have Y, each of the third and fourth men would also know what color he had [see above]. So I still don't know whether I have R or Y.

(At this point no more information can be obtained by the first and second men. So Case I is not possible, from [4].)

Case II

First man:	I have R or X [from axiom].
Second man:	I have R or Y [from axiom].
Third man:	I have R or Y [from axiom]. If I have R, first man would know he had Y; he didn't know, so I have Y.
Fourth man:	I have R or X [from axiom]. If I have R, second man would know he had X; he didn't know, so I have X.
First man:	I have R or X. If I have R, fourth man would know he had X [from axiom]; and third man would know he had Y because second man didn't know he had Y. If I have X, each of the third and fourth men would also know what color he had [see above]. So I still don't know whether I have R or X.
Second man:	I have R or Y. If I have R, fourth man would

know he had X because first man didn't know he had X; and third man would know he had X [from axiom]. If I have Y, each of the third and fourth men would also know what color he had [see above]. So I still don't know whether I have R or Y.

(At this point no more information can be obtained by the first and second men. So Case II is not possible, from [4].)

Case III

First man: I have R or X [from axiom].

Second man: I have R or X [from axiom]. If I have R, first man would know he had X [from axiom]; he didn't know, so I have X.

Third man: I have R or Y [from axiom]. If I have R, second man would know he had X because first man didn't know he had X. If I have Y, second man would also know what color he had [see above]. So I don't know whether I have R or Y.

Fourth man: I have R or Y [from axiom]. If I have R, third man would know he had Y; he didn't know, so I have Y.

First man: I have R or X. If I have R, third man would know he had Y because second man knew he had X; he didn't know, so I have X.

Second man: (Already knows.)

Third man: I have R or Y. If I have R, fourth man would know he had Y [from axiom]; then first man would know he had X because fourth man knew he had Y. If I have Y, each of the fourth and first men would also know what color he had [see above]. So I still don't know whether I have R or Y.

(At this point no more information can be obtained by the third man.)

Then *the third man asked failed to name the color of his hat*.

The Dart Board

From [1] and [2], each of Alma, Bess, and Cleo scored 11.

From [1], [4], and [5], Bess and Cleo cannot both have lied because both of their hypotheses cannot be true at the same time—the first person to score in the triangle is simultaneously the first person to score in the circle, and vice versa. So, from [6], either Alma and Bess both lied or Alma and Cleo both lied.

Suppose Alma and Bess both lied. Then, from [1] and [2] and the false conclusions in [3] and [4], either:

(i) Alma scored two 4s and one 3, and Bess scored one 3 and four 2s; or

(ii) Alma scored one 5 and two 3s, and Bess scored one 3 and four 2s. But, in both i and ii, the hypothesis in [4] cannot be true, from [1]. So Bess did not lie. So Alma and Bess did not both lie.

Then Alma and Cleo both lied. Then, from [1] and [2] and the false conclusions in [3] and [5], either:

(iii) Alma scored two 4s and one 3, Bess scored three 3s and one 2, and Cleo scored one 5 and three 2s; or

(iv) Alma scored one 5 and two 3s, Bess scored two 4s and one 3, and Cleo scored one 3 and four 2s.

In iv the hypothesis in [5] cannot be true. So Cleo did not lie in iv. So Alma and Cleo did not both lie in iv, and iv is not the correct situation. So iii is the correct situation and *Cleo scored the 5*.

Because Alma and Cleo both lied, the hypotheses in [3] and [5] are true; so, from [1], Alma scored one 3 in the square before Cleo scored the 5. From iii, the conclusion in [4] is true (that Bess must have told the truth is confirmed); from [1] and iii, the hypothesis in [4] is false.

Index

(Solutions in italics)